BARBARA JOHNSON

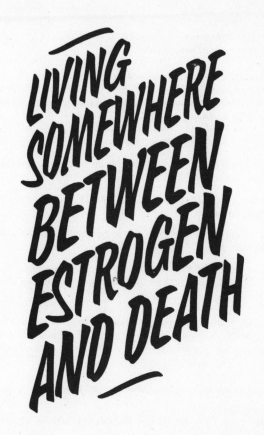

W PUBLISHING GROUP™

www.wpublishinggroup.com

A Division of Thomas Nelson, Inc.
www.ThomasNelson.com

W Publishing Group
Nashville, TN

Unless otherwise indicated, Scripture quotations used in this book are from the Holy Bible, New International Version (NIV). Copyright © 1973, 1978, 1984 International Bible Society. Used by permission of Zondervan Bible Publishers. Other Scripture references are from the following sources:

The King James Version of the Bible (KJV).

The Living Bible (TLB). Copyright © 1971 by Tyndale House Publishers, Wheaton, Ill. Used by permission.

The Message (MSG). Copyright © 1993. Used by permission of NavPress Publishing Group.

The New King James Version (NKJV), copyright © 1979, 1980, 1982, 1992, Thomas Nelson, Inc., publisher.

The New American Standard Bible (NASB), © 1960, 1962, 1963, 1968, 1971, 1972, 1973, 1975, 1977 by the Lockman Foundation. Used by permission.

Many of the jokes, maxims, and quips included in this volume have been contributed by friends of Spatula Ministries, and in many cases it has been impossible to identify the original source. Appropriate attribution will be made in future printings if the creators' identities become known.

Library of Congress Cataloging-in-Publication Data

Johnson, Barbara (Barbara E.)
    Living somewhere between estrogen and death / Barbara Johnson.
        p.   cm.
    Includes bibliographical references.
    ISBN 0-8499-3653-5
    1. Aged women. 2. Aged women—Anecdotes. 3. Aging. 4. Old age.
I. Title.
HQ1061.J545   1997
305.26—dc21
                                                    97-1635
                                                    CIP

Printed in the United States of America.
4 5 6 7 8 9 PHX 28 27

To Gopher Bill,
my perfectionistic engineer husband.

I call him my joy-robber, but the truth is he has made me look so hard to find the hidden joys in life that I've found *more* joy than I ever dreamed possible! He is the solid, practical anchor who keeps his airhead wife grounded; I love to hear him say I'm his best friend. He's my invaluable helper, facilitator, and coworker, and without him none of my books would ever have been completed.

Contents

The Wonder Years

*When we wonder how we got this old
and why we didn't save for a facelift!*

Bill and I went on a cruise recently that left us both feeling younger than our years—and exhausted too! When our tour group assembled on the first day and we got a chance to look each other over, Bill and I were surprised to discover that we were apparently the youngest ones there! When you consider that we're no spring chickens (closer to Geriatric Junction than we like to admit), you can imagine how old those other folks looked!

I wondered if the trip had been described as a senior citizens special somewhere in the fine print (which we never read because neither one of us can *see* fine print anymore). But we weren't upset about it. At first it was sort of fun to be the "youngsters" of the group; I figured that would give me an excuse for any mischief I might get into.

1

But by the second day, the newness of being "young again" had worn off as the flip side of the situation became obvious. Every time we left the boat for some sort of bus excursion, again and again we heard:

"Uh-oh! I left my sweater back on the boat."

"Has anyone seen my pocketbook? Oh, no . . . I must have left it in the restroom."

"I can't see a thing without my glasses. I must've put 'em down when I looked through those pay-binoculars back at the scenic view."

After each one of these announcements, all the old eyes seemed to turn expectantly to Bill or me. Sagging faces would wrinkle up into a hopeful smile. "Oh, honey, that's so nice of you to go get it for me," they would say as Bill or I heaved a patient sigh and headed back to retrieve the lost items.

We assisted them as they slowly hobbled up and down stairs; we waited outside restrooms holding their purses, scarves, sweaters, totebags, and half-eaten sandwiches entombed in fast-food boxes. After every stop, we loudly guided them as their feet struggled to find the steps of the bus. "Just a little higher . . . okay . . . good . . . up a little more . . . you're almost there. That's it." And then we pushed and shoved to get them to the top of the steps and back to their seats.

Then, back on the bus, we suffered through the same sort of confused conversation with at least one of them:

"Here you go! Here's your seat."

"Are you sure this is my seat?"

"Yep, this is it, all right. Just scoot on in, and we'll be on our way."

"It sure doesn't *feel* like my seat . . . I had mine fixed just right, and this one is tilted back too far."

"Well, just lift that little lever and—oops! Too fast. Your teeth still in?"

"I don't think this is my seat. I was sitting closer to the front. Now I can't see anything."

"No, you were right here. You'll be able to see as soon as

Marcus takes off his hat. See? Here's your crocheting, and there's Agnes's magazine that you borrowed."

"That's my crocheting? I thought I was making a pink *sweater.*"

Finally, everyone would be seated—usually with one or two of them still fussing that someone else had their seat and a few not even certain they were on the right bus—and off we'd head for our next stop, where we'd go through it all over again.

At mealtimes, Bill and I read the menus out loud for our companions, who couldn't seem to make heads or tails of it. We cut up their meat, spread mayonnaise on sandwiches, fetched extra napkins, and tracked down the hot water to dilute too-strong coffee.

Sometimes when one of these feeble, confused, white-haired tourists was asking for help, I'd smile what I hoped was my patient-looking smile and hope the old lady couldn't read my mind, which wanted desperately to say, *For goodness' sake! This is so simple. Can't you figure this out for yourself?*

Of course when these feelings got close to the surface, I would stuff them back inside.

Not too long after this "vacation," Bill and I headed out on a speaking engagement, this time to Canada. In Montreal we boarded a tiny plane (it only held twelve people) to fly to the city in Quebec where I was to speak. As we boarded the plane we were given a rather complicated form having to do with customs legalities as we crossed the Canadian border.

The paper didn't make any sense to me; I looked at it until I was cross-eyed and still couldn't make heads or tails of it! Meanwhile, out of the corner of my eye, I could see a darling little white-haired lady across the aisle rapidly filling in the blanks on her form.

In frustration, I sighed, huffed, clucked my tongue, and tapped my pencil on the irritating paper. But she didn't look up, too busy writing out her own answers on the form. Finally I admitted loudly, "I can't *read* this. How can I fill it out?"

The old lady smiled patiently then returned to her writing

as she said slowly, as though I would have trouble hearing her, "Well, the first line is asking your *NAME*. The next line is for your *ADDRESS*. The third line is your *BIRTHDAY* . . ."

Dutifully I wrote down my name and address as she instructed. We were halfway through the confusing form, with the old lady carefully pronouncing the information each line wanted. At that moment, I felt old, feeble-minded, and confused. How could this be so difficult for me when she was whizzing through her form like a court stenographer? I paused and sighed again. Then I said, "You're so smart. Now, what does this next line want?" And then I added, "Thank you for helping me with this."

She smiled that same patient smile again. She told me later she was eighty years old. She reached across the aisle and gave my arm a little pat. "Oh, I'm glad to help," she said. But in her twinkling eyes at that moment, I could read her mind. It was saying, *For goodness' sake! This is so simple. Can't you figure this out for yourself?*

It was at that moment, however, that she actually looked over and saw my form.

"Oh, honey. You're on the *French* side. If you'll just turn the paper over, the other side is in *English!*"

We had a good laugh over that incident, and that darling gal taught me a valuable lesson that day: Old age depends more on how you feel and act than on how many years you've lived. That charming old lady had several years on me, but my inability to figure out the form made me feel decrepit while her good-natured laughter made her seem like a breath of fresh air.

Living Joyfully . . . Deep in Denial

The fact is, I've always said I don't really like being around old people—so it's a little tough realizing that *now I AM one!* It's easy for me to slip into the mind-set that portrays most of them as being like that group of befuddled senior citizens on our cruise: endlessly forgetful, hopelessly confused, and, in general, a pain to be around. When that image comes to mind,

I can't help but whisper a prayer, begging, *Please, please, PLEASE, Lord! Don't ever let me be old!*

Of course the only way to avoid getting old is to die young, and that just wasn't God's plan for me. If you've read my other books, you know there were times when I *wanted* that to happen; I argued with God that I'd suffered enough and it was time for me to come home and get some heavenly rest. But He apparently had other things in mind for me.

They say that the best way to grow old is not to be in a hurry about it—and Lord knows, I've put it off as long as I could. But the other thing about old age is that it happens to us without any effort at all on our part. We blow out the candles on our twenty-first birthday cake, and *poof!* The next thing we know, we're wearing goofy party hats and singing "Auld Lang Syne" in some old folks home in Florida and wondering, *How did this happen?*

Laughing through the Ages

Yes, according to my birth certificate, I am living somewhere between estrogen and death, or, as someone said, between menopause and LARGE PRINT! But I don't have to *act* my age because, thank God, I've discovered a wonderful anti-aging remedy. It won't actually turn back the clock, and it's certainly not a new wonder drug. In fact, it's been promoted since biblical times as a cure for a wide variety of problems (see Proverb 17:22). And it's no secret, either; lots of people use it. *(They're* the ones I'd like to take my next cruise trip with!)

If you know anything about me, or if you've read any of my seven other books, you can already guess what I'm talking about. It's the same God-given gift that's kept me functioning through some previous tragedies.

What is it?

Laughter.

A sense of humor.

An attitude expressed by Oscar Wilde's motto: "Life is too important to be taken seriously."

A tendency to look for joy throughout the journey, to find a way to laugh at *everything* life throws my way—even death. How could anyone laugh at death? Well, consider what the late Dorothy Parker suggested for the epitaph on her own tombstone:

Excuse my dust.[1]

Don't you love it! This is the same attitude that caused comedian Bill Cosby, as he approached his fiftieth birthday, to laugh when he quoted his grandfather's advice, "Don't worry about senility. . . . When it hits you, you won't know it."[2]

For Better or For Worse by Lynn Johnston

For Better or For Worse © Lynn Johnston Prod., Inc.
Reprinted with permission of Universal Press Syndicate. All Rights Reserved.

That attitude is the same sparkling joy that *other* old lady shared with me on the little plane in Canada as we laughed together about my struggles with the silly customs form. That wonderful eighty-year-old "youngster" reminded me that our age truly is just a number, nothing more. It's how we feel inside that determines how old we really are.

It's the way we live our lives—our attitudes and our actions—that determines what stage of life we're in. You may have a husband in the throes of a midlife crisis, parents who are struggling to remember what decade they're in, and adult children who are giving you fits, but if you can keep breathing and laughing, you'll survive (at least until it's *your* turn to move into the home for the bewildered and try to remember what decade it is!).

Anyone can laugh—whether you're mobile or bed-ridden, active or lame, whether you're equipped with single or double eyes, arms, ears, legs, and kidneys! No physical limitation can prevent you from laughing. Even if some problem has robbed you of your voice, you can still laugh with your eyes. And if for some reason your eyes can't sparkle anymore, you can still smile in your heart.

Laughing at Life

My all-time, tried-and-true method for lightening up any situation is to laugh at it! Fortunately, I have a lot of kindred spirits out there who share their funny experiences with me, including hilarious stories about their health problems.

One of my favorites is about a daughter who was concerned that her elderly mother hadn't had a Pap smear in several years. She finally persuaded her mother to let her make an appointment for an exam with her own doctor. "You can spend the night with me, and I'll drive you to his office in the morning," she told her mother. "Then we'll go out for a nice lunch."

The mother reluctantly agreed and spent the night in her daughter's apartment. The next day they went together to the doctor's office, and while the daughter waited in the lobby the mother nervously undressed, climbed up on the table, and, with the nurse's assistance, slid her heels into the stirrups.

The doctor came in, greeted her pleasantly, then settled onto his stool.

"My, aren't we FANCY today!" he exclaimed as he lifted the sheet draped over the old lady's upraised knees.

Shocked, she had no idea what the doctor meant. When the exam was over, she hurriedly got dressed and rushed out to meet her daughter in the waiting room. In a panic, she repeated what the doctor had said.

"What in the world do you think he meant by that?" the mother asked, bewildered.

"I have no idea, Mother. What did you do to prepare for the exam?"

"Well, I showered, and I used some of that feminine deodorant spray in your bathroom," the mother replied.

There was a slight pause as the woman looked her mother in the eye.

"I don't HAVE any feminine deodorant spray, Mother."

"Yes you do—that tall pink-and-gold can."

"Mother! That's not deodorant. That's *gold-glitter hairspray!*"

That charming old lady sure gave that doctor's day a lift, didn't she? Of course she didn't really mean to . . . but that's what makes the story so funny!

Some people spread joy wherever they go—whether or not they mean to! And some of us have to put forth a little effort to keep a smile in our hearts. Others are never happy unless they're complaining about something. I got a note from a woman who had a friend like that. Luckily, the woman who wrote to me could see the humor even in having such a pessimistic friend. She wrote, "My friend Irene is *always* complaining! I took her to a greeting-card store the other day, and she looked and looked and looked.

"Finally, I said, 'Irene, what in the world are you looking for?'

"She replied, 'I'm looking for a card that says, "I had what you've got—only WORSE!"'"

This is the same witty woman who told me her horoscope

predicted one morning that she was going to have an adventure involving water. "And then," she continued, "I dropped my false teeth in the toilet!"

Surviving the Change

It's easy to find things to complain about as we grow older, but it's so much healthier to *laugh* instead. Of course, sometimes it's not easy to *find* those laughable situations. One of the least funny things about growing older is menopause.

With our hormones raging, our emotions swinging wildly

"Having nine lives is cool, but if I have to go through menopause again, forget it!"

to and fro, our memory shot, and our bodies flashing with enough heat to bake the Thanksgiving turkey, we NEED to laugh—but often find ourselves crying instead.

I'm not sure how a MAN could ever understand menopause, but I think Dave Barry came pretty close when he wrote this hilarious definition:

> [The change] is the stage that a woman goes through when her body, through a complex biological process, senses that the woman has reached the

stage in her life where her furniture is much too nice for her to have a baby barfing on it. So the body stops producing estrogen, which is the hormone that causes certain distinct female characteristics such as ovulation and the ability not to watch football.

This bodily change is called "menopause," from the ancient Greek words *meno* (meaning "your skin sometimes gets so hot") and *pause* (meaning "that it melts Tupperware").

Also some women tend to become emotional and easily irritated by minor things that never used to bother them, such as when their husbands leave a partly used meatloaf sandwich in bed, as though the Meatloaf Sandwich Fairy were going to come along and pick it up for him.

The traditional way to cope with menopause is to ask your physician to prescribe costly pharmaceuticals, but of course these can cause harmful side effects. . . . So more and more health experts are recommending a "holistic" approach, in which you develop a deeper understanding of the natural process that your body is going through and then, with this newfound knowledge as your guide, you stick the meatloaf sandwich into the breast pocket of your husband's best suit.[3]

An article in *Today's Christian Woman* put a really uplifting slant on menopause. Citing Ecclesiastes 3:1—"There is a time for everything, and a season for every activity under heaven" —it said:

Menopause is a season, not a disease. It's not fatal. In fact, it's a good time to take stock. In the same way that a harsh winter is always followed by spring and new life, menopause can be a precursor to a fresh beginning to the rest of your life. Take time to reflect on what you did *right* the first two-thirds of your life, and dare to dream about your next twenty-five years or so.[4]

Lambasting the Labels

If you're like me (that is, if some people would consider you to be *old* too), you dislike those labels the rest of the world wants to put on us, even the one that says we're no longer old—we're "chronologically gifted"! No matter how well-intentioned they are, these names just seem to go from bad (old people, senior citizens, golden agers, and mature Americans) to worse (elderly, geezers, seasoned citizens, and old biddies).

And I know I'm not alone in resenting being categorized this way. My eye doctor, Dr. Robb Hicks, was kind enough to share an anecdote about this problem of "name-calling" that occurred within the medical profession.

After surgery one day, Dr. Hicks joined another doctor in the hospital physicians lounge, where they had gone to wash the surgical powder off their hands, look for donuts, and then dictate their patients' medical records into the recording system while the procedures they had just completed were still fresh in their minds.

The other physician, "Dr. Tom," had just been given a birthday card signed by all the surgical nurses "congratulating" him on reaching his sixtieth birthday. He feigned pleasure over the attention, but back in the physicians lounge with his friends, Dr. Tom was obviously not excited about reaching this milestone.

The doctors settled into their cubicles to dictate the medical reports. Dr. Hicks heard Dr. Tom begin dictating the history and physical status of the patient whose gallbladder he had just removed:

"This well-nourished Caucasian *elderly* man . . . ," Dr. Tom began. Then he paused for a few seconds. Dr. Hicks heard a slight sigh, and then Dr. Tom backed up the recorder and commenced again: "This well-developed, well-nourished Caucasian man *of sixty-two years* . . ."

Like Dr. Tom, I don't want to be thought of as elderly. Instead, I want to be like those women described by another physician, plastic surgeon Harvey Austin, who said, "There is no such thing as an old woman! We've been conned. My [plastic surgery] patients are not vain. They only want to let the little girl out!"[5]

GOD IS ONE OF
THE ELDERLY

ED FISCHER

© 1991 by Ed Fischer and Jane Thomas Noland. Reprinted from
What's So Funny about Getting Old? with permission of Meadowbrook Press, Minnetonka, MN.

That's us, isn't it? We're not old; we're just mature little girls. We have a little something extra, now that we're heading toward the sunset. Unfortunately, that little something extra is often in the worst possible place. I love the little quip that says,

> With age a woman gains wisdom,
> maturity, self-assurance . . .
> and ten pounds right on the hips.[6]

When I go around the country speaking for conferences, I often say, "Actually, I'm a perfect ten under here. I just keep it covered with fat so it doesn't get scratched!" For many of us that perfect-ten body is attached to a thirty-year-old mind encased in an antique display case! As Ashleigh Brilliant says,

> Inside every older person,
> There's a younger person,
> Wondering what happened.

> Ashleigh Brilliant
> Pot-Shot 1390, © 1978

No matter how incongruously our youthful minds fit into our aging bodies, we can refuse to be old. We can celebrate our youth—no matter how many decades we've been youthful!

For Women Only!

Before we go any further, I need to make one small request. If you're a man, would you please stop right here? Don't turn another page. I don't mean to hurt your feelings, but, you see, this book is FOR WOMEN ONLY! So just close the cover and put the book back where you found it. If you're a man and you bought this book without noticing the warning right there on the cover that says FOR WOMEN ONLY! (in bright letters) and if you don't have a wife, mother, sister, or friend to give it to, then you have my permission to return this book to the store where you bought it. Just show the salesclerk your receipt, hand over the book, and say, "Barbara says on page 13 that I'm not allowed to read this book, so would you please give me my money back?"

If they're reluctant to give you a refund, try whining. This usually works.

It's not that there are any big secrets hidden in these pages. And except for the chapter that pokes fun at men in my usual *kind and educational way*, there's nothing controversial here—no putdowns or backstabbing. It's just that, well, I'd like to talk about *women* things in this book. That's why we put *estrogen* right there in the title. Testosterone problems are NOT for us!

© Dana Summers. Reprinted with permission.

Actually I've looked forward to writing this book for several years, but I never felt old enough! My previous books have been aimed at hurting parents who have suffered a loss through death or a broken relationship; those books contain many experiences shared by families who are part of Spatula Ministries, the organization Bill and I started many years ago. Spatula's goal is to peel hurting parents off the ceiling with a spatula of love and set them on the road to recovery.

In writing those earlier books, I always felt I had to share my "credentials," my own painful experiences. But while I was doing that, in the back of my mind I was thinking, *Oh, it would be so nice just to write a book for the sheer fun of it and not have to include my credentials!*

Finally, I realized that if I wanted to write that kind of book I'd better do it now—while I can still remember what I wanted to say! So here it is, a book of zaniness that pokes fun at the way many of us are right now: frazzled by life's knock-out blows, staggering down that inevitable road to the home for the bewildered, fighting fifty or enduring our sixties—but still looking for those little splashes of joy that brighten our pathway like transient diamonds.

If you're one of the estimated forty-three million women "in peri-menopause (the term designating the transition phase between having regular periods and no periods at all), in menopause, or past menopause,"[7] this book is for you. We're in or nearing that stage the late Margaret Mead whimsically described as the "PMZ: post-menopausal ZEST"![8] Actually, I prefer to think of it as a time that's ripe for post-menopausal ZANINESS!

Think of this book as a cookbook of PMZ "recipes." You won't find any sad stories here, no harrowing tales of brokenness. This book is just a journal of joy. Sometimes it makes sense; sometimes it doesn't. My goal is not to help you lose twenty pounds, control your raging hormones, or find the right hairstyle for your funeral debut; instead I just want to share some bursts of joy with you. And I'm not just talking about mindless giggles here, either. I mean the kind of humor my friend Marilyn Meberg talks about—humor that releases us "from the bondage of our circumstances and ourselves so that the inherent capacity to laugh, which lives in us all, can bubble to the surface and carry us through those times that are tension-producing and spirit-breaking."[9]

If I *do* feel the need to remind you that I'm offering this light-hearted encouragement after a lifetime of "tension-producing and spirit-breaking" experiences, I hope you'll just let me blurt out some code words for heartache, perhaps DYNA-ANGINA! Then you can pause to remember my credentials—and we'll get back to our silliness.

Part of the goofiness I plan to share has grown out of a story included in an earlier book, *Mama, Get the Hammer! There's Fly on Papa's Head!* The story, from an unidentified newsletter, described a modest woman trying to buy a box of Tampax at a supermarket. As luck would have it, she picks up a box with no pricetag, and the cashier makes a storewide announcement on the PA system, asking the stock person to look up the price. The stocker misunderstands and thinks the cashier is talking about *thumbtacks*. He asks, again on the PA system, "Do you mean the kind you push in with your thumb or the kind you pound in with a hammer?"

I loved the story but was reluctant to put it in my book. After all, this is not a subject one would expect in a book written for hurting parents by a post-menopausal woman! I was afraid the shock might be too much for some folks.

But just the opposite happened. Of all the stories in all the books I've written, that tampon story is one of the favorites that's often mentioned by readers when I'm out on speaking appearances. If I've heard it once, I've heard it a zillion times: "I *loved* that story about the Tampax! I laughed 'til I cried!"

And then the women say, "Have you heard . . . ?"

That's where the next round of "female" stories came from—jokes, quips, and real-life stories that women could only tell to other women.

For example, at one meeting I mentioned the tampon story—then added that that kind of experience would never happen to me now because I'm living "somewhere between estrogen and death, or, to put it another way, between the *Blue Lagoon* and *Golden Pond!*" A woman came up to me afterward and said, "Barbara, we're living *somewhere between training bras and support hose!*"

But then another woman added the clincher: "Let's face it, Barb," she said. "We're living *somewhere between Tampax and Depends!*"

Then, along those same lines, someone else showed me a greeting card with suggestions for what to do with a diaphragm you no longer need. One of the suggestions was to use it as a "rainhat for a cat"![10]

Girl-Talk

That's the kind of silliness you're gonna find in this book. I think you'll agree these aren't *naughty* jokes and stories—you won't find any foul language in these pages; there's certainly nothing here about immorality. The things I want to share are, well, personal. Girl-talk. Jokes and anecdotes from women about women that are just too good not to share.

When we were putting this book together, I tried out a few of the jokes on the folks at Word Publishing, asking, "Could I put this in the book?" Then, I suppose, a memo probably went throughout the corporate offices: "Barbara Johnson wants to know if it's okay to talk about tampons and adult diapers in her next book."

Next I asked, "Could this book be just for women?"

I've already caused those good folks more headaches than they deserve. It seems every time we agree on a new book project, I throw out some ridiculous request, and somebody somewhere within the organization—usually the one with the most common sense and the greatest experience—says, "Why, we can't do *that!*"

But, as I said earlier, I've found that whining works wonders. In the end, they've always had the kindness (and courage) to do things my way. So this time, when I asked if we could put the disclaimer on the cover, they just rolled their eyes, said their prayers, and hoped for the best. And the result is right here in your hands. I hope you have as much fun reading it as I've had in collecting all these little jewels of joy and putting them together for you!

I've figured out why people get gray hair.
It's from worrying about their teeth falling out!

Some women fight old age until the day they die. Lady Nancy Astor said, "I refuse to admit I am more than fifty-two, even if it does make my sons illegitimate."[11]

Fulfilling a friend's request that he scatter her husband's ashes from a small airplane, the Rev. Robert Fulghum dutifully carried the ashes aloft and tossed them out the open door of the little plane—only to have the wind send the ashes right back in the door, "filling the cockpit with the final dust of Harry, the deceased husband. Covering the widow, the pilot, and me," he wrote in his book *Uh-Oh*. "We flew back to the field in silence. . . . I can now add a practical paragraph to the *Minister's Manual*: 'If the ashes of the deceased are blown back into the cockpit, return to the airport and borrow a vacuum cleaner from the airport janitor and vacuum the deceased from the plane. NOTE: It is *very* important first to put a clean bag into the vacuum cleaner!'"[12]

Being tickled to death is a great way to live. Jumping for joy is good exercise.[13]

Signs you're getting old:
Dialing long distance wears you out.
You know all the answers,
but nobody asks you the questions!

You know it's time to throw in the towel
when you'd fall apart completely
if it weren't for static cling![14]

Many people's tombstones should read:
"Died at thirty. Buried at sixty."

Nicholas Murray Butler

There are three stages of life: youth, maturity, and
"My, you're looking good!"

President Dwight Eisenhower[15]

Those who love deeply never grow old; they may
die of old age, but they die young.

—English playwright
Sir Arthur Wing Pinero

Age gracefully? I think not! Age ferociously
instead. Seize everything valuable within reach.
Extend. Question. Give. The face will follow. All the
cosmetic surgeons in the world could never pro-
duce such a face.[16]

You know you're getting older when . . .
"Happy Hour" is a nap!

People who need to get older
Are much luckier
Than people who need to get younger!

Ashleigh Brilliant,
Pot-shot 2927, © 1983

A feeble, elderly woman, all hunched up and using a cane, limped into a doctor's office. Five minutes later, she came out, walking erect and without a limp.

A guy in the waiting room asked, "Gee, what did the doc do? You're doing just great."

The lady replied, "He gave me a longer cane."

Overheard at the beauty shop: "I knew her forty years ago, and she looked just like she does today: OLD!"

Stop the Conspiracy!

Have you ever noticed that when you're over the hill, everything seems *uphill* from where you are?

Stairs are steeper. Groceries are heavier. And *everything* is farther away. Yesterday I walked to the corner and was dumbfounded to discover how long our street had become.

And that's not all. People are less considerate now, especially the younger ones. They speak in whispers all the time, and if you ask them to speak up, they just repeat themselves, endlessly mouthing the same silent message until they're red in the face and exhausted. What do they think I am, a lip-reader?

And they drive so fast you're risking life and limb if you happen to pull onto the freeway in front of them. All I can say is, their brakes must wear out awfully fast, the way I see them screech and swerve in my rearview mirror.

Even clothing manufacturers are becoming less civilized these days. Why else would they suddenly start labeling a size 6 dress as a 12? Do they think no one notices that these things no longer fit around the waist, hips, thighs, and bosom?

The people who make bathroom scales are pulling the same prank but in reverse. Do they think I actually *believe* the number I see on that dial? Ha! I would *never* let myself weigh that much!

Just who do these people think they're fooling? I'd like to call up someone in authority to report what's going on—but the telephone company is in on the conspiracy. They've printed the phonebooks in such small type that no one could ever find a number there!

All I can do is pass along this warning: Maturity is under attack! Unless something drastic happens, pretty soon *everyone* will have to suffer these awful indignities.

Courtroom lawyer, questioning a potential juror:
Q: Have you lived in this town all your life?
A: Not yet!

Once you pass forty, your "big break" will probably be a bone.[17]

Beauty is only skin deep . . .
but fortunately, I have very deep skin.

Ashleigh Brilliant,
Pot-shot 4614, © 1988

"As far as the east is from the west, so far has He removed our transgressions from us." (Ps. 103:12 NASB)
Now, if God would just do that with our gray hair and wrinkles, we'd be in great shape!

Nancy L. Jackshaw[18]

If you can read these words without a magnifying glass, you have no business reading this book! You're obviously much too young and probably wouldn't understand the humor anyway! Go buy a comic book and come back in thirty years!

What's the difference between a terrorist and a menopausal woman?
You can negotiate with the terrorist!

Lord, deliver us from war, pollution,
and cellulite buildup.

© 1989 Remarkable Things,
Long Beach, California

Bumper Sticker:
SO MUCH WORK . . . So few women to do it.

No wonder I feel so tired—
I'm older now than I've ever been before!

Ashleigh Brilliant
Pot-shot 358, © 1972

Real Life Adventures by Gary Wise and Lance Aldrich

The first time you're offered a senior citizen discount.

Sign posted in a customer service department:
Suppose we refund your money,
send you another one without charge,
close the store, and have the manager shot.
Would THAT be satisfactory?!

You were taught, with regard to your former way of life, to put off your old self, . . . to be made new in the attitude of your minds; and to put on the new self, created to be like God in true righteousness and holiness. (Eph. 4:22–24)

Fat Farm Failures . . .
and Other Excuses for the
Middle-Age Spread

*You have a heart of gold. That would explain
why you weigh two hundred pounds!*

After I had a hysterectomy several years ago, my doctor assured me it was just a myth that women automatically put on extra weight after menopause. "There's no reason why you should gain weight if you eat a sensible diet and get suf-icient exercise," he said. The problem is . . . eating sensibly has never seemed like much fun to me!

For nearly a year after my surgery, I steadily gained a pound or two every month. My friend Mickey was experiencing the doctor's idea of the "myth" in the same way. So he and I decided we were never going to lose weight on our own; instead, we agreed we would splurge and have ourselves admitted to a fat farm—a spa located some fifty miles north of Los Angeles, out in the desert. Friends warned us we wouldn't get much to eat at this place, so we stopped at a fried chicken restaurant on the way for a bucket of reinforcements. We also took crackers and snacks in our luggage and sneaked everything into our room at the spa.

Sure enough; our friends were right. The food wasn't just scanty—it was almost microscopic! It did have nice names, however, like souffle of this and fillet of that. They served a lot of weak tea and fancy little cubes of gelatin with fingernail-size portions of whipped cream. One especially memorable dessert was called "tofu supreme."

We would have starved except for the fried chicken and crackers we ate in our room that first day. For dinner that night they served a small wedge of lettuce and a spoonful of fluffy yogurt.

The next day we had veggie burgers. Have you ever had a veggie burger? At this fat farm, a veggie burger was two very THIN oblong crackers with some strands of carrots, a pile of ground-up broccoli, and some bean sprouts smashed between the crackers! As we studied this sorry excuse for a lunch, Mickey and I had fun wondering what McDonald's might name this concoction if it were added to their menu. I thought they might call it the McSprout or the McSproccoli. Mickey opted for the Quarter-Ouncer.

But just thinking of McDonald's when our stomachs were so desperate for some real nourishment (that is, something fried and fattening) made us want to make a break for the nearest golden arches (which were at least a half-hour's drive away). So we couldn't play that game for long!

We were all expected to dress up for dinner each night. So there we sat, looking beautiful and starving to death. We were supposed to stay for four days, but the fried chicken only lasted until the first night, and we ran out of crackers and cheese the next afternoon. It was then that we decided to escape that place while we still had enough energy to make the drive home.

On the way back to LA we stopped at that same fried chicken place. Faint with hunger, we staggered up to the window and ordered the REALLY big bucket.

When someone sent me the following menu, it reminded me of those two long days at the fat farm. I don't know where it came from, but I think you'll quickly see why it's "guaranteed" to make you lose weight:

MONDAY
Breakfast: Weak tea
Lunch: Bouillon cube in 1/2 cup water
Dinner: 1 pigeon thigh
             3 ounces prune juice (to be gargled only)

TUESDAY
Breakfast: Scraped crumbs from burnt toast
Lunch: 1 doughnut hole
Dinner: 2 canary drumsticks

WEDNESDAY
Breakfast: Boiled-out stains of tablecloth
Lunch: Bellybutton from navel orange
Dinner: Bee's knees and mosquito knuckles

THURSDAY
Breakfast: Shredded eggshell skins
Lunch: 1/2 dozen poppy seeds
Dinner: 3 eyes from Irish potato (diced)

FRIDAY
Breakfast: 2 lobster antennae
Lunch: 1 guppy fin
Dinner: Fillet of soft-shell crab claws

SATURDAY
Breakfast: 4 chopped banana seeds
Lunch: Broiled butterfly liver
Dinner: Jellyfish vertebrae

SUNDAY
Breakfast: Pickled hummingbird tongue

Lunch: Prime ribs of tadpole
Dinner: Tossed paprika salad
       Aroma of empty custard pie plate
Note: All meals are to be placed under a microscope while eaten—
to make them more filling.

Source Unknown

Obviously, Mickey and I were big failures at abiding by the rules; instead, we decided to leave the fat farm and farm our fat ourselves! We probably shouldn't have gone together, because neither one of us had enough will power, when it came to food, to turn down a single morsel. We reminded each other of the friend Erma Bombeck described when she said it was just her luck to go to a fat farm and share a room "with the only person there who had sewn Reese's Pieces into the hem of her jacket."

**"My burger's still a little pink on the inside.
Hold the cigarette lighter up to it for a
couple of minutes, would ya?"**

Since then, I've been very good about watching my weight. I watch it go up and down and up and down. I heard someone call this "the rhythm method of girth control!"

Actually I *do* watch what I eat—until I get it in my mouth; then I lose sight of it.

The Portly Majority

The only good thing about being plump, or well-upholstered, as I like to say, is that we're not alone. Despite all the diets, weight-loss clinics, fitness clubs, and self-help books, *millions* of us are overweight. In fact, the results of the most recent National Health and Nutrition Examination Survey show that "for the first time, overweight people outnumber normal-size ones in the United States."[1]

THIS IS NOT YOU AND IT'S NOT ME...

BUT JUST LOOKING AT HER MAKES ME FEEL BETTER.

Well, to those of you living "in the fat," I say, *Hang in there!* It may be true that "your bellybutton should not be touching your knees when you're standing,"[2] but there are ways to disguise your flab. You could always learn to alter your clothes so they fit your body more comfortably. But one problem with that, as Erma Bombeck predicted, is, "If you get a dress to fit your hips, you have enough material left over from the hem and sleeves to slipcover Brazil."[3]

Another alternative is the new body slimmers (the things we used to call corsets and girdles). And get this: In addition to squeezing your thighs, derriere, and torso into excruciatingly tight undergarments that are two sizes too small, you can now wear a girdle to control bat-wing arms. Someone sent me a newspaper clipping that described it as "a Lycra band to slip onto your arm and make it look firm under all those snug-fitting dresses and blouses."[4]

Totally Distracted

It just doesn't seem fair, does it? By the time we've reached this age, we've survived so many trials, failed at so many diets. About the only one I could ever follow was the Stress Diet.

Breakfast
1/2 grapefruit
1 slice whole wheat toast
8 oz. skim milk

Lunch
4 oz. broiled chicken breast
1 cup steamed zucchini
1 Oreo cookie
herb tea

Midafternoon Snack
Rest of the package of Oreos
1 quart rocky road ice cream
1 jar hot-fudge sauce

Dinner
2 loaves garlic bread
large pepperoni and mushroom pizza
3 candy bars
entire frozen cheesecake eaten directly from the freezer

Pamela Pettler[5]

This silly regimen reminds me of the diet Erma Bombeck described. She said, "One January I went on a seven-hundred-calorie-a-day diet. By the end of the month, I had eaten all my allotted calories through June 15." Erma liked to say that in two decades she'd lost "a total of 789 pounds. I should be hanging from a charm bracelet."

"It's a low-cholesterol ice cream cone— a scoop of mashed potatoes with sprinkles."

Food Links

Now that we've passed the halfway point in life, many of us could use a breather—a brief respite between the exhaustion of getting our children to adulthood and the prospect of dealing with our parents' (or our own!) slide into la-la land. Sure there are other sources of comfort available to us: We could call a friend, go for a walk, or read our favorite passages of Scripture. But in all likelihood, our friend would have a new recipe to share, and if you're like me your favorite place to walk is to the donut shop! And, while Scripture is certainly a balm for my soul, it can also be a stimulant to my appetite. Maybe that's how some beloved passages get contorted like this one:

The Twenty-Third Cupcake

My doctor is my shepherd; I shall not weigh more.

He maketh me to lie down in green sweatpants; he ordereth me to do situps. He specify-eth my goal. He sendeth me down jogging trails of endless length for my heart's sake.

Yea, though I stroll by the door of the bake shop, I will not enter; my sweetrolls and crumbcake I secretly buy elsewhere.

I eatest my cupcakes in the presence of no one. I feast on rich Twinkies and Ding-Dongs. My cup's full of ice cream.

Surely huge hips and thunder thighs will haunt me all the days of my life, and I will live in a body of cellulite forever.

Ann Luna

You see, for some of us, everything we do reminds us of food, even reading Scripture! Or we see a baby's cute little toesies, and we think of bite-size Tootsie Rolls. We notice the wrinkles in an old man's smile and think of prunes. We pull our pantyhose over our thighs and think of cottage cheese. We gaze at majestic, snow-capped mountain peaks and see chocolate-marshmallow sundaes topped with whipped cream. And every time we look at the night sky we think of Milky Ways and Starbursts. It never ends! We can't even look at a traffic light in December without wondering whether the red and green M&Ms are in the stores yet.

A Fanatic for Food

It's a constant challenge for me to keep my mind off food—but I'm not quite as bad as those people who equate eating with a divine encounter! In a newspaper interview one person said, "Food is the closest thing to God because it brings everyone together and puts a smile on everyone's face."[6]

Another expert, the director of an eating disorders center, said, "For many women, loving food has become safer than loving a man. Food never breaks a date, doesn't criticize or reject you."[7] No wonder when we think of a "gorgeous hunk" these days the image of a refrigerator comes to mind! But that brings to mind the little quip someone sent me. It says:

> Diet Rule #2:
> Never weigh more than your refrigerator.[8]

We love to eat—but there's a downside: a big backside! So we go on a diet, but if food is "the closest thing to God" and "safer than loving a man," when we diet we're not just declining a second helping of mashed potatoes—we're destroying our whole psyche! Maybe that's why a fitness trainer put his finger right on the problem when he astutely announced:

> One of the problems with diets is the first
> three letters spell "die"![9]

Food can easily become the center of our lives, and when we try to break its hold on us, we sometimes feel like we're coming as close to death as we want to get on this side of the pearly gates!

You Know It's Time to Diet When . . .

There have been times in my life when I didn't worry about

"You weighed yourself on three scales and
none registered over 63 pounds?
Your diet must be working."

my weight; I had plenty of other worries to distract me! But
now that Bill and I have settled into our golden years, there
are fewer distractions—and more tempting things to eat.

And we may soon be tempted to eat even those things
we've never liked—because now they're being genetically
engineered to taste like something we *do* like. I read somewhere that scientists have already developed green peppers
that taste like apples. Next they may try to make Brussels
sprouts taste like grapes.[10] If only they could make strawberry
shortcake taste like anchovies and sweetrolls taste like
Limburger cheese—now *that* would be helpful to us perpetual
dieters!

There's rarely any good news about my favorite foods these
days. But someone did send me some wonderful news about
asparagus the other day (and I love asparagus!). It said, "Your

body expends more energy digesting asparagus than it takes in—four spears have thirteen calories, no fat, and considerable nutrients."[11] Now *that's* something to celebrate!

Unfortunately, asparagus is not the main staple of my diet. And although I don't *think* I'm overeating, and even though I try to be careful about making the right choices, somehow, like old age, the extra pounds just seem to magically appear. One day we're a sleek, size 10 glamour girl, and the next thing we know we're the mother of two kids, the grandmother of five, and the final resting place for about ten million fat cells! That reminds me of a little note sent to me recently by a friend who, like many of us, is constantly struggling with her weight. She said, "The beaded belt I wore years ago around my hips is now my necklace, and my rear end looks like an inflated parachute." Still, this darling woman can laugh at these challenges. In the note she said our friendship makes her "fat cells vibrate with laughter."

This lighthearted attitude seems to be the best alternative when it becomes obvious that those fat cells are *not* transients—somehow they're trying to take up permanent residence on our bodies. For many of us, that's a moment of great revelation—THE moment when we know it's time to diet. Some of the other indicators, according to clippings friends have sent me, are:

- You take a shower and nothing below your waist gets wet.

- You get a pedicure and have to look in a mirror to see what color the manicurist painted your toenails.

- You get out of breath just blinking your eyes in bright sunlight.

- Your finger gets stuck in the holes of the telephone dial.

- Tollbooth operators on the expressway suggest that next time you use the lane marked "WIDE LOADS."

- On hot days, small children flock to you to stay in the shade.

- Bus drivers ask you to sit up front to serve as an airbag for the rest of the passengers in case of a crash.

Losing Weight without Losing Your Mind

Actually, experts say that weight control is quite easy if you keep in mind these first two rules of successful dieting:

> There are only two things you need to avoid in order to lose weight: *food and drink!*

And . . .

> If it tastes good, spit it out!

If those guidelines are just a little too stringent for you, consider this more reasonable advice from Dr. Gabriel Cousens, a California physician and author of *Conscious Eating*, who suggests that at mealtime you eat a few bites with your eyes closed and focus on the food in your mouth. Focus on enjoying the meal "instead of considering it another task to be done efficiently."

I think Dr. Cousens's advice may be especially appropriate for us older folks, because many of us now have the luxury of time to try his suggestions. Most of us no longer have to eat in a rush; our days of holding the steering wheel in one hand and a Big Mac in the other while trying to control a rowdy Little League team in the back of the minivan are (we hope) over. So if we're eating in a hurry these days, it may be because it's a habit rather than a necessity.

Missing Motivators

Perhaps one reason why we women tend to gain weight in our later years is that we've run out of motivation. In past years, we went on crash diets for our prom, graduation, or

YOU'VE HEARD OF THE ESTROGEN PATCH?

© 1997 Barbara Johnson.

NOW THERE'S SOMETHING NEW... THE DIET PATCH!

wedding, then we tried to shed a few pounds for our children's baptism, twenty-five-year homecoming celebrations, or family reunions. But when all of those milestones are behind us, we develop other priorities—breathing, for example, or trying not to lose our minds while we wrestle with parents who need to be in a nursing home but refuse to go, or holding our families together when one of us struggles through a health crisis.

Sure we'd like to be thinner, but it just isn't happening. At that point, we have two options:

1. Lie.
2. Learn to live with it.

Despite Christian teachings, a lot of women choose the first alternative. In fact, a recent newspaper article said, "More of us lie about our weight (34 percent) than anything else—shaving off a few pounds to make ourselves feel better." If this is your choice, you might as well fudge a little on your age while you're at it. According to the same article, 20 percent of all American women do![12] If ever I have to give my weight, I just say, "I weigh one hundred and *plenty!*"

A woman has reached middle age
when the only pinches she gets
are from her girdle!

I like to think of banana cream pie as a fruit.

Pat Prints calendar, 1993

EXERCISE AND DIET
TO FIGHT HAZARDOUS WAISTS!

Class Reunion

My class reunion's coming,
    and I don't know what to do.
My weight and chins have doubled
    since the year of '42.

I look into the mirror and—
    Good grief! How can this be?
Gray hair, false teeth, thick glasses—
    It's my mother's face I see!

But I head out to the party.
    No sense moping, I decide.
I'll just have to grin and bear it.
    (But I'm dying, deep inside.)

Then I walk into the banquet hall
    And stop. There's some mistake.
Not a single classmate do I find.
    Did I confuse the date?

Still, the faces seem familiar,
    As each one I keenly stare at . . .
Then I realize I'm looking at—Good grief!
    My classmates' parents!

Ann Luna

A Dieter's Malapropisms:
    It's on the fork of my tongue.
    Take it with a bag of salt.
    May a mighty oak grow from these tiny mustard
seeds of faith.

You can't have your chicken and eggs too.

People who live in glass houses shouldn't throw sour grapes.

How to Plant a Special Garden

First, plant five rows of peas: Preparedness, Promptness, Perseverance, Politeness, and Prayer.

Next to them, plant three rows of squash: Squash Gossip, Squash Criticism, and Squash Indifference.

Then five rows of lettuce: Let us be faithful, Let us be unselfish, Let us be loyal, Let us be truthful, Let us love one another.

And no garden is complete without turnips: Turn up for church, Turn up with a smile, Turn up with determination.[13]

Keep smiling!
The luscious plum forgot to—
and became a wrinkled prune.[14]

Wouldn't it be wonderful if there were a delicious, "all-natural" food that is nutritious, fat-free, has no cholesterol, and promotes good health?

There is! You'll find it described in Galatians 5:22–23—the "fruit of the Spirit." This fruit is wholesome and beneficial—and it's even better when shared![15]

Middle age
is when you choose your cereal
for the fiber,
not for the toy.

I've reached the age
where it's harder and harder
to think of my body as a temple.
(It's more like a building project
that got out of control!)

If there is a fountain of youth,
it is almost certainly caffeinated.[16]

Beauty is skin deep,
but stupid goes all the way through.[17]

No one is lonely while eating spaghetti.
It requires too much attention!

I'm not fat . . .
I'm calorically gifted!

The cheerful heart has a continual feast. (Prov. 15:15)

A Fact of Aging:
What You Lose in Elasticity
You Gain in Wisdom

*It's not that I'm against exercise.
It's just that when I look at my body
I feel it's already been punished enough!*

Until a few years ago, my favorite thing to exercise was my right to vote! The only time my heart rate got into the "workout zone" was while I was waiting in the checkout line, nervously wondering if I'd have enough money to pay for all the groceries I'd piled in the cart for Bill and our four perpetually hungry sons. My idea of *strenuous* exercise was, as someone said, to fill the tub, pull the plug, then fight the current!

It's not that I sat around grooming my collection of dust bunnies or eating bonbons. As the years have gone by, Bill and I have stayed busy by traveling for speaking appearances and running Spatula Ministries. We used to get our weight-training experience by delivering industrial-size bags of catfood for a ninety-year-old neighbor lady who had thirty-five cats and was no longer able to go to the store herself.

Actually, I thought we were in pretty good shape. No, we weren't going to be asked to pose as models for any fitness gyms, and you won't find my portrait in that new pinup calendar that features shapely models who've lived at least half a century, but we managed to meet the World Health Organization's definition of fitness: We were "able to meet the challenges of daily life."[1] That attitude changed when I was diagnosed a few years ago with adult-onset diabetes. At that

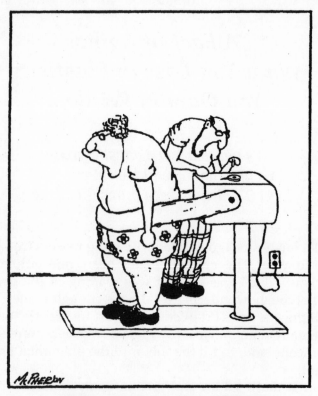

"You want it set on low, medium, high, or industrial strength?"

point, exercise—*real* exercise—suddenly took on new impor-
tance. My doctor told me exercise was absolutely essential if I
planned to stay attached to all my fingers and toes.

Somehow I just couldn't see myself squeezing my sixty-
year-old body into one of those svelte leotards and jogging off
to a gym. There had to be another way. Finally I came up with
what seems to be the perfect solution—for me, at least.

When we're at home, the things that consume most of my
time are the mail and the telephone. The mail to Spatula
Ministries is delivered in big rectangular tubs that we pick
up at the post office. (I've decided our address should be a
post office TUB number, rather than a box number, because
BOX sure doesn't describe the barrel-size bin where our mail
ends up.)

Because it's so much faster, I try hard to respond to as
many letters as possible with a phone call instead of a letter.
That's lots of phone calls! But while I'm on the phone, I'm also
on my exercise bike. (So if you get a phone call from me someday and I sound a little out of breath, it's *not* because I've
exhausted myself dialing those long-distance numbers, as
some jokester said about old people.)

Bill set up my exercise bike in my Joy Room, an addition to
our mobile home that's filled with funny plaques, pictures,
toys, gadgets, dolls, and all manner of hilarious stuff folks have
sent me over the years.[2] As I pedal my bike, I enjoy all those
goofy things in the Joy Room while talking on the phone.

While I'm riding the bike, I'm also touring the country—
making imaginary trips along a big, colored map of the
United States Bill posted on one wall of the Joy Room in front
of the exercise bike. As I cycle along, I stick a pushpin into the
map every twenty-five miles so I can keep track of how many
miles I've accumulated. Seeing those pins march across the
map helps keep me motivated! It's been a couple of years now
since I started this routine, rolling out of our home here in
California while staying put right in my Joy Room. I try to
ride the bike ten to fifteen miles every day we're home, so by
the time you read this, I should be closing in on Philadelphia!

But following a cross-country route is not the only thing I do to stay motivated. On a table by the exercise bike I keep a list of Spatula friends so that, as I near a city, I can look to see who lives there. Then I pray for that person, asking God to be especially close to her that day and to wrap her in His big comfort blanket of love and let her feel His presence that day.

My goal is to cover all fifty states this way. (It might take awhile to pedal to Alaska and Hawaii, but I'm determined!) As I look at the route on the map and check my address list to see who lives along the way, I also pay attention to the weather reports. If the weather is cold, I may put on some earmuffs—just to get into the spirit of things; as I cross the desert I may sip iced tea while I pedal along.

This method works for me. While I strengthen my heart and lungs I'm also strengthening my spiritual life—putting some zing into my conversations with God by praying for specific friends (maybe one of them is YOU!).

Find Something Fun to Do

Of course, my system won't work for everyone—and I don't follow the same routine every day. Sometimes I ride a *real* bike; Bill and I even have a tandem bicycle we pedal around the neighborhood. (The problem with this is that Bill rides in front and can't really tell what's going on behind him, so it's tempting for me to just relax and enjoy the ride without putting out much effort!)

As many of you know, we live in a mobile home park where there are lots of retired folks (some of us are more retired than others). One day I was out riding my ten-speed around the park and stopped to let a little old white-haired lady cross the bike trail. As she hobbled in front of me, she smiled and said, "My, honey, it's sure nice to see someone around here with dark hair for a change!"

Of course, she didn't know that I call my hair my "convertible top." No one else besides my hairdresser and God knows what's underneath! But the old lady's comment lifted my spirit and made me feel much younger than my years. That's one advantage of exercising out in the neighborhood— I may encounter someone who offers a friendly hello or a word of encouragement.

So now, in the same way that dear little lady's comment motivated me to keep going, I encourage you to exercise so you can enjoy these later years in life. The experts say that exercise has more than just physical benefits; it not only helps us control our weight and maintain good circulation, it also adds to our sense of well-being by helping us fight stress, be hopeful, and stay young at heart.

Dr. James Rippe, author of *Fit Over Forty*, says, "It's hard to find a better prescription than staying physically active and optimistic." Staying active, he says, improves our chances for a healthier, more enjoyable life.[3]

You might be surprised to discover how easily you can work moderate exercise into your daily routine. If you can't picture yourself pedaling an exercise bike, consider working out with one of those large rubber bands while you talk on the phone. You can find them at most sporting-goods stores, and they're usually less than ten dollars for a package of three. Just loop one end of the band around your foot and hold the other loop in your hand, and you can work your leg and arm muscles while you're working your jaws! (Just be sure to take it off before you try to get out of your chair so you don't fly through the house like you've been fired out of a slingshot!)

Even washing windows or waxing the car is good exercise, if you happen to enjoy that kind of thing. If you don't stay too long at the bargain tables, shopping can be beneficial too. And of course, dancing is another way many older people get their exercise. All over the country, gray-haired dancers are breezing through classes at places ranging from Dance Masters to Jazzercise.

One of the easiest but most effective ways to exercise is just to walk. Experts say this (and most other forms of exercise) are especially effective after dinner. By exercising after your evening meal, they say, you not only burn extra calories, you get yourself out of the house, where you might be tempted to settle onto the sofa and continue eating as you watch TV.

Know the Enemy!
There's a little quip that says:

> Over the years, I've learned who is my friend and who is NOT my friend.
> GRAVITY is NOT my friend!

Well, for some of us, that sofa is the enemy too! A newsletter from the Baylor College of Medicine in Houston said, "The most exhausting part of exercising is the mental argument that takes place when you try to talk yourself into getting up off the couch and *just doing it!*"[4] Remember: "All glory comes from daring to begin."[5]

But *when* to begin? That's the question. I love columnist Dave Barry's answer to that perplexing question: "Not today, certainly. You've done enough today! I would rule tomorrow out, also, seeing as how it comes so soon after today. You rush into these things, and the next thing you know you've strained a ligament or something. So I would say the best time to begin would be first thing after Easter, although not the one coming up."[6]

Barry also points out another advantage of exercise you may not have realized: A growing familiarity with PAIN!

> People who exercise regularly are prepared for . . . pain. Take joggers: you see them plodding along, clearly hating every minute of it, and you think, "What's the point?" But years from now, when you're struggling to adjust to the pains of the aging process, the joggers, who have been in constant agony for 20 years, will be able to make the transition smoothly, unless they're already dead.[7]

All right, now. That's enough foolishness. Let's get back to the challenge at hand: finding a form of exercise that works for you. Remember, it doesn't even have to involve activities that have traditionally been considered exercise. For example, one article I saw said that even *fidgeting* can play a role in keeping off the pounds. That's terrific news for those restless types who can't sit still for more than a minute without popping up to water a plant, straighten a picture, or adjust the mini blinds.

I'll bet you never realized you were becoming more fit while you fidgeted! But that's possible. The article said that researchers from the National Institutes of Health estimated that "people who paced the room, moved arms and legs frequently, or changed seated positions burned 138 to 685 extra calories per day."[8]

INSIDE ME THERE'S A THIN WOMAN STRUGGLING TO GET OUT...

BUT I CAN USUALLY SEDATE HER WITH 4 OR 5 CUPCAKES!

There's a new-fangled idea that just might be more appealing than fidgeting. It's called belly-rolling, and while I haven't tried it yet, it *sounds* like something that could certainly make me laugh whether or not it works as a fitness aid.

The gadget is a GIANT, sturdy ball about three feet in diameter that's supposed to be a real boon for "those who haven't worked out in a while or have back problems." According to one report, it's used to increase flexibility and strength, especially in folks in their forties and fifties. One way to use it is to "drape yourself over the ball, facedown, arms at sides, knees bent, toes touching the floor, and ball positioned directly beneath the midsection. Hang there thirty seconds or more, allowing back and shoulders to stretch and relax. Exhale and gently lift head and chest until completely off ball, holding two to three seconds."[9]

Just picturing myself draped over that giant beachball makes me laugh. It's so easy to imagine all sorts of silly scenarios—like the ball rolling over with me still attached to it, arms and legs flying out in every direction, clearing a broad path through our mobile home park! Now THAT would give the old folks something to talk about around the shuffleboard court!

Blazing Birthdays

Sometimes, as hard as we try to stay in shape, birthdays still take their toll on us. And other times, birthdays themselves can be disastrous, as this silly letter describes:

Dear Esther,

I'm sorry you couldn't make it to my recent birthday party. Apparently, it was quite an event—not that I remember much about it.

They tell me the problems started when I drew in a big breath to blow out the eighty-four candles someone had set afire on top of my birthday cake and, blinded by the glaring blaze and disoriented by the merciless heat, I forgot why I was holding my breath and temporarily lost consciousness.

Luckily, my daughter and her family had decided to host the party beside their swimming pool, so instead of breaking my hip in a disastrous fall to the kitchen floor, I toppled backward into the pool. The water was so cold, I instantly awakened from my faint, screaming at the top of my lungs and, as a result, losing my dentures in the deep end of the pool.

Without a moment's hesitation, my nephew Joey

dived in and swam to the bottom to retrieve my teeth, but when he tried to resurface, he accidentally became entangled in the billowing fabric of my tent-shaped housedress, and together we kicked and flapped and squawked, undulating repeatedly until my wig finally let go and floated off, ghost-like, in the churning water.

Thinking one of her puppies was drowning, the old dog Sparky jumped in next, swimming deter-minedly into the fray to rescue the wig.

It was about that time that my birthday cake, with all seven dozen candles still burning, suddenly ignited like a sparkler and set the paper tablecloth on fire.

Fortunately, the firefighters arrived within min-utes, and if the firetruck had been hauling water I suppose everything would have turned out okay. But the truck's tanks were empty, so one of the firefighters, his yellow rubber coat popping and squeaking loudly as he ran, dropped a pumper hose in the pool.

I thought for sure he would rescue us, as we were still flapping and squawking in the icy water, but Sparky apparently mistook him for some sort of monster—perhaps a loud and lurching fire hydrant—and she suddenly began barking so fero-ciously that the poor man dropped the hose and never looked back. He said later he wondered why the old dog was so zealously guarding that undu-lating mass of inflatable beach toys.

Eventually, the pumping lowered the water level in the pool until our feet could touch bottom. But by then the whole backyard was a swirling vortex of flames and smoke. I couldn't see a thing, what with all the haze and chaos—and the fact that one lens of my bifocals had popped out when I hit the water. But Sparky obviously has either sharp eyesight or a keen memory despite her many years. She took off like a rocket after that same poor firefighter and took a big chunk out of his thigh before he scrambled up the only tree in the yard that wasn't burning.

I guess Joey and I looked a little bedraggled as we groped our way out of the pool and through the swirling curtain of smoke and chaos. We tried to slip, unseen, out of the growing crowd, but the firefighters mistook us for arsonists trying to avoid detection and quickly called the police, who were already in route in response to another call about a crazed and rabid dog wreaking havoc on our property.

I tried to explain what had happened, but since Joey had left my dentures back in the pool, no one could understand a word I was saying. They hauled us both off to jail, bringing Sparky along as a material witness.

It was nearly midnight before my daughter and her husband finally came to bail us out. I was surprised when they dropped me off at the YWCA, saying I would have to stay there for a little while. It was a little sad to think I had completely missed celebrating my birthday.

I hope you're doing well. Please give my regards to everyone at the nursing home. I'll try to give you plenty of notice next year so you can join me for a piece of birthday cake—if my daughter's house is rebuilt by then.

Gertrude

Look in the Mirror

A lot of us are at that awkward age when Father Time starts catching up with Mother Nature. We can always claim that old age is about ten years older than we are, but let's face it: We're at that point in life when everything starts to wear out, fall out, or spread out.

Sometimes I'm tempted to adapt a line I see every day on my car and transpose it onto the full-length mirror in my bedroom. It would say:

IMAGES IN MIRROR ARE SMALLER
THAN THEY APPEAR.

You see, just like so many things, fitness and exercise are affected by our attitudes about ourselves. As someone said, "Attitude is the mind's paintbrush. It can color any situation."

When you look in the mirror, you can still see your smooth, unlined face just the way it was twenty or thirty years ago—unless, that is, you insist on wearing your glasses while you're looking in the mirror! (Let's face it, many of us have eyesight that's deteriorating faster than our faces!) The point is, don't be too hard on yourself. And look on the bright side. That's the attitude of the woman who reported that she looked in the mirror each morning and said, "Thank you, dear Lord, that wrinkles don't HURT!"

The Older the Better

There are a lot of things that can make you feel old, and looking into the mirror (if you're wearing your glasses and the WRONG attitude) is one of them. But there's good news. An article I saved from several years ago suggests if we can get past sixty-five, we usually feel BETTER about getting old. It's that stretch between sixty and sixty-five that seems to be the problem.

For example, one study showed that significantly more people between ages sixty and sixty-four visit the doctor than those who are sixty-five to sixty-nine. It seems that people in their early sixties are nearing the transition time that will pole-vault them into retirement. They begin to feel age "creeping up on them," and they start worrying about their health.

This theory says that how old you feel also depends on who you spend your time with. People in their early sixties may still be dealing quite a bit with younger friends and peers, particularly in the workplace, and they may feel slower than those who are in their fifties or even younger. But when retirement happens, people over sixty-five tend to spend more time with those their own age, and they're comfortable with that group because, in many cases, they may even feel a bit stronger than their peer group.[10]

Maybe it's all a matter of perception. At sixty you can get up in the morning and decide you feel weak "because you're getting older." But at sixty-six, you get up in the morning and conclude that you feel pretty good for your age.

Stay Flexible

This choice illustrates the two basic ways we can deal with aging: Negatively, by letting it wear us down, or POSITIVELY, by choosing to see how the pluses far outweigh the minuses. One way to deal positively with the advancing years is to stay as fit as we possibly can. And, of course, it always helps to be able to laugh. As Ashleigh Brilliant says,

> Life becomes much easier,
> once you get through
> youth, middle age, and old age.

> Ashleigh Brilliant
> Pot-shot 2584, © 1982

When you're old, the challenge is not in bending down to touch your toes.

It's in remembering what you're there for once you arrive.

Two old ladies in a rest home were talking. One of them said to the other, "It's my birthday. I'm eighty years old, and, by George, I want to do something shocking, so I'm going to streak the cafeteria today."

Sure enough, she runs by the cafeteria with nothing on.

Two old men, eating sloppy joes, see her. One of them says to the other, "Say, Alma's jogging clothes are looking kinda wrinkled today, aren't they?"[11]

Erma Bombeck said when she went to sign up for an exercise class, they told her to wear loose clothing.

"I said, 'Are you kidding? If I had any loose clothing I wouldn't need to take the class!'"

They say life begins at fifty.
It begins, all right—
it begins to DISINTEGRATE!

It's tough to be at the age at which,
when you go all out,
you end up all in.

Remember, you may be OLDER today than you have ever been before, but you are YOUNGER than you will ever be again!

Time may be a great healer . . .
But it's a lousy beautician!

I've reached that point in life where
the only thing I can exercise is CAUTION!

Great news: Laughing one hundred times is the physiological equivalent to working out on a rowing machine for ten minutes! The problem is, once I get going, I'm afraid I won't be able to stop, and I'll laugh myself into anorexia![12]

Thank you for calling the Weight Loss Hotline. If you'd like to lose half a pound right now, press 1 eighteen thousand times.[13]

At our age, forget the natural ingredients.
We need all the artificial color and
preservatives we can get!

The show is really over when you find yourself picking your teeth out of the popcorn.

Finish each day and be done with it.
You have done what you could;
Some blunders and absurdities no doubt crept in.
Forget them as soon as you can.
Tomorrow is a new day;
You shall begin it well and serenely.

Ralph Waldo Emerson

WOMEN: It's easy to go for the burn—
just sit around and wait for a hot flash.

Those who hope in the LORD
    will renew their strength.
They will soar on wings like eagles;
        they will run and not grow weary,
        they will walk and not be faint. (Isa. 40:31)

Growing Old Is Inevitable;
Growing Up Is Optional

Wild in the spirit—twinges in the hinges.

To tell the truth, I didn't pay a lot of attention last year when news reports said American astronaut Shannon Lucid was breaking the world record for a woman in space. But when she came back home after spending more than six months aboard the Russian space station *Mir*, I was awestruck by the pictures.

Fascinated, I watched as Dr. Lucid waved to the crowds as she returned to Florida. Later, I watched again as she was greeted by the president upon her arrival back in Houston. While the rest of the world was probably marveling at her courage and intelligence, I watched it all and couldn't get over one wonderfully startling fact: *SHANNON LUCID HAS GRAY HAIR!*

Of course, that was after 188 days in space. I'm not sure *what* color her hair was before she moved in with the Russians! But that's not the point. The wonderful thing is that when most people think of astronauts they think of YOUNG, athletic daredevils with movie-star looks and cocky attitudes. Instead, here's the holder of an incredible space-endurance record, and SHE'S A MIDDLE-AGED WOMAN!

Shannon Lucid set this extraordinary record at the age of fifty-three on her FIFTH mission into space! So I hope she continues to let that gray hair show; I hope she's still breaking space records when she becomes a grandmother. It's such an inspiration for the rest of us who are over fifty and, like Shannon Lucid, continue to face challenges.

In the welcome-home ceremonies, President Clinton said when Shannon was in eighth grade, she told her teacher she wanted to be a rocket scientist. Her teacher replied that "there was no such thing and that if there were it wouldn't be a woman," the president said.[1]

Keep on Dreaming!

In these later years of our lives, some of us may be confronted by the kind of long odds and tall roadblocks that little Shannon ran into when she shared her dream with that rather narrow-minded teacher. In the same way, it may seem that we're running out of time to accomplish the dream we have for ourselves. Perhaps we're starting to think it will never be anything more than a dream—and that even if the dream were "do-able," someone else would *do* it, not us. After all, we may tell ourselves, we're getting on in years, and dreams are for younger people.

For many women in what I like to call "the second half of our first century," the challenge is not to accomplish some life-long dream but just to cope, to survive one more day. During these years, we may be struggling with children who are still giving us fits even though they're adults, or maybe we're trying to survive the loss of a child. Many women in this age bracket have parents whose health—or sanity—is fading, and

they're also coping with husbands who are enduring all these same problems plus their own midlife crises. Or we may be dealing with a break in a family relationship due to death, divorce, or alienation of some sort. Or perhaps you're at a point when life seems to be whizzing by and leaving you in the dust. Maybe just getting up in the morning is a challenge for you.

Well, here's a statistic that should nudge you right off that mattress and onto your feet: "In an ordinary year, about 130 Americans—or one out of every two million—will die from falling out of bed. Over the same period, one out of four hundred will be injured just lying in bed, generally because of the headboard collapsing, the frame giving way, or some other mechanical failure!"[2]

Tight Corner by Ken Grundy and Malcolm Willett

GRUNDY & willett 11-9   © 1995 Grundy/Willett Dist. by Universal Press Syndicate

When catching a falling star, make sure it fits in your pocket.

See? You're not safe in bed anyway, so you might as well get up and get going. Climb up out of your rut, pull yourself upright—and do something courageous!

As I was accumulating material for this book, I tagged the folder for this chapter "risk-taking" because that's what I'm urging you to do in these pages: Be bold, take a chance, do something different, push back a barrier, or, in those cases when you think you're at the end of your rope, KEEP BREATHING! Whether it's something as simple as attending church again after a lapse or something as potentially frightening as dating again after your marriage ends due to death or divorce, I hope you'll take a good look at what's left of your life and choose to make it meaningful.

Choose Life

The sentiments expressed by the late Douglas MacArthur still hold true today. He said, "Whatever your years, there is in every being's heart the love of wonder, the undaunted challenges of events, the unfailing childlike appetite for what comes next, and the joy of the game of life. You are as young as your hope, as old as your despair."

In other words, it's your choice. You can choose to "grow young" and hopeful—or you can wallow in your despair and age quickly. I know it's scary to take risks, to try something new, because we can't help but wonder, *What if we fail? What if we get into this and realize we've made a HUGE mistake?* Well, you have to figure . . . at this point in your life, this won't be the FIRST mistake you've ever made, and no matter how bad it is, it probably won't be the WORST mistake you've ever made. And unless you fail at something REALLY adventurous (like swimming the English Channel or attempting an Evel Knievel–style motorcycle jump over the Grand Canyon), it probably won't be your LAST mistake, either! And in all likelihood, what you GAIN in wisdom, experience, and character by taking this risk will far outweigh any problems that occur, even if things don't go exactly as you hoped. And you'll become a better person for having tried.

Somewhere I saw a line that said:

THE PERSON WHO RISKS NOTHING
DOES NOTHING, HAS NOTHING, IS NOTHING!

Max Lucado puts it this way:

> Life has rawness and wonder. Pursue it. Hunt
> for it. Don't listen to the whines of those who have
> settled for a second-rate life and want you to do the
> same. Your goal is not to live long; it's to live.
> Jesus says the options are clear. To be safe, you
> can build a fire in the hearth, stay inside, and keep
> warm and dry. You can't get hurt if you never get
> out, right? You can't be criticized for what you
> don't try, right? You can't fail if you don't take a
> stand, right? . . . So don't try it. Take the safe
> route.
> Instead of building a fire in your hearth, how-
> ever, you can build a fire in your heart. Follow
> God's impulses. Adopt a child. Move overseas.
> Teach a class. Change careers. Run for office. Make
> a difference. Sure it isn't safe, but what is?
> You think staying inside is safe? Jesus disagrees.
> "Whoever seeks to save his life will lose it." Reclaim
> the curiosity of your childhood. Just because you're
> near the top of the hill doesn't mean you've passed
> your peak.[3]

Laughter Brings Blessings

Many older women, especially those who suddenly find
themselves alone, hesitate trying something new because
they might look foolish. Thank heaven for braver souls—
like the friend of Spatula Ministries who had a very clever
and generous idea for helping her church raise money for a
new building. At a "service auction" held by the church
fund-raisers, she sold eight singing telegrams, which she

merrily "delivered" for the purchasers. Then something magical happened:

> Soon I began receiving calls. I went to the post office for a sixtieth birthday. To the park for an aunt's eightieth birthday. To a nursing home to sing for a mother's eightieth birthday, and so on. The more I went out the sillier I dressed. Usually I used the same song but individualized it for the occasion. Everyone received me so graciously and I had great fun. Laughter brings such blessings!

Now, you know this darling gal probably felt foolish the first time she arrived at the post office and announced that she was going to SING for someone! But she overcame those fears and earned a blessing while spreading joy to others.

The Magical Mix of Laughter and Tears

Risk-takers' lives are enriched, not just by the joy we experience, but also by the tears we shed. Remember, it takes both sunshine and rain to make the rainbow. That's a principle of life the Disney studios discovered when they began making feature-length animated cartoons.

One of the first such cartoons, *Snow White,* was a huge commercial success, but subsequent animated features didn't do as well. When the Disney experts analyzed failures and compared them to *Snow White,* they discovered that "the films that people would pay to see again and again had two ingredients—laughter *and* tears! Everything they did from that point had to have both elements before it was released."[4]

Don't be afraid! As one writer said, "Confident people are not afraid of suffering, for suffering brings experience, and experience, wisdom. Sufferings of this present time will seem insignificant as we keep our eyes on the future."[5]

Step out in faith and do what you feel led to do, whether it's something simple, like volunteering for a new outreach ministry with your church, or something more complicated—like applying for astronaut training!

And if you need help in venturing out of your shell, here are ten steps that will help give you a friendly little boost of confidence—a gentle push out the door—as you set off on your journey:

1. Begin the day in a calm and cheerful mood. Say, "This is going to be a good day. I will be calm and cheerful today."

2. Try smiling at others. A smile is contagious and you will feel better as others smile at you.

3. Count your blessings. List them one by one. Do you ever realize the real wealth you have?

4. Enjoy this day with beautiful thoughts, pleasant memories. Live life one day at a time.

5. Be adventurous. Try walking and see new neighborhoods, new buildings and parks, new scenery.

6. Give a friend a phone call or write a letter. Let that person know he or she is in your thoughts and prayers. Offer a word of encouragement— the oxygen to the soul.

7. Be a happy person. See the bright side of life. Having a cheerful, loving attitude lends itself to your best health.

8. Do a good deed or give something beneficial to a loved one.

9. Give of yourself; offer your services to a hospital or church. Help people. The law of giving will reward you tenfold.

10. Do the best you can each day. You are really living only when you are useful and constructive.[6]

Stepping Out in Faith
My life has been sprinkled with many kinds of "risks"— mostly ridiculous pranks I've pulled to ward off my own

brushes with insanity! One of them occurred back in 1980 when the beautiful Crystal Cathedral was about to open here in Orange County, California. Dr. Robert Schuller had invited several dignitaries to be a part of the dedication ceremonies: Billy Graham, Los Angeles mayor Tom Bradley, the late Norman Vincent Peale, and opera singer Beverly Sills, to name a few. It was a very elaborate event, and admission was by invitation only.

We had a houseguest at that time—Andy, a darling college student who was visiting us. He had read all about the big, gala event, and he said to me, "Let's go!"

I explained that in no way could *we* ever get in because it was for dignitaries—important folks and invited guests—not little peons like us. But he was determined to get in; he even made a bet with me that he could figure out a way to get us *both* inside.

We drove down there—it's just about a fifteen-minute ride from our home—and parking was almost impossible. We had to leave the car far down the street and walk back to the entrance. The ceremonies were just about to commence; flags were fluttering high, and the orchestra was playing as the VIP guests were being seated in their special places of honor.

In my purse I carry a little telephone beeper that clicks and whirs to let me retrieve telephone messages when I'm away from home. Andy had seen me use it; as we neared the front entrance, he asked for the gizmo. Then, grasping it firmly in front of him, he hurriedly approached a red-coated usher who had been greeting guests and passing out programs at the front door.

With me hurrying to stay up with him, Andy stepped up close to the usher and said in a low tone that only she could hear, "We're from security, and we have to check out the platform for a possible bomb."

Immediately the usher hustled us inside the door, and we proceeded at a rapid pace down to the front of the Crystal Cathedral, where the audience was eagerly anticipating the beginning of the program. Andy thrust the little beeper into the potted palms and flower arrangements situated around the platform, pressing the clicker to make it beep. He moved around with a concerned look on his face while I struggled not to laugh. After all, we were in plain view of *everyone* in the audience, and we were *definitely* not dressed for this! Andy was in blue jeans and a sport shirt, and I was wearing slacks and a blouse.

After several beeps and clicks with his head down in the planters, Andy whirled around to signal a thumbs-up to the startled usher, who had returned to the door. Then he briskly walked back up the aisle and out the side door, with me hot on his heels. I did spot a few familiar faces in the audience as we retreated; their bewildered expressions nearly did me in. It was all I could do to keep from guffawing as we tripped back up the aisle. But I managed to get outside before we both erupted into gales of laughter—and Andy quickly reminded me that he had won the bet.

Now, before we go any further, I need to say emphatically that security at the Crystal Cathedral today is very sophisticated; it would be impossible now to do what Andy and I did that day. Someone trying to pull off such a prank would be courteously escorted to a holding room until the authorities could come and transport him to the nearest mental hospital!

The really amazing thing is that the Crystal Cathedral has welcomed me many times since then; in fact, I've been invited to speak at women's conferences there, and my Spatula group has been meeting there regularly for the past twelve years! A couple of years ago, I was the guest on *Hour of Power*, a nationally televised program from the Crystal Cathedral that airs every Sunday morning. Decked out in a big straw hat covered with red geraniums, I was interviewed by Dr. Bruce Larson, who talked about my book, *Stick a Geranium in Your Hat and Be Happy*. He told the audience about three of my books being on the bestseller list at that time, and he spoke supportively about our work with hurting parents.

As I stood there, looking out over that vast audience and taking in the beauty and the overwhelming spectacle of that glorious place, suddenly an image ignited my mind: Andy and I, nosing through the palms on the edge of the platform, looking for fictitious bombs. If you ever see a tape of that interview, you'll see that I appear to be on the verge of uncontrollable laughter at one point in the program—that's when I remember Andy's and my first visit to that fabulous place.

Dr. Schuller has been most kind to our ministry in the years since the Crystal Cathedral opened. Recently he wrote me a letter, congratulating me on the success of my last book, *I'm So Glad You Told Me What I Didn't Wanna Hear*. He ended the letter by saying, "Your life is blessed to be a blessing!"

What a wonderful phrase—"blessed to be a blessing." Surely if this is true then I'm expected to take a few risks here and there to make sure that blessing gets passed on! That thought pushed me to risk saying yes to an "extra" invitation I received last year when Bill and I were in New Orleans for a conference. Usually when we travel the timing is pretty tight and we don't have any free time for side trips, but a Spatula friend had heard I was going to be speaking in New Orleans, and she called and asked if we could come to her small town in Mississippi and join her and her husband for lunch.

Her hometown is more than a two-hour drive from New Orleans, so arranging a quick visit wasn't easy. But she is a precious friend who has been through a difficult loss, and I was delighted to be able to arrange our schedule so we could have lunch with her.

When we arrived at her home, we were expecting a quiet, simple lunch with just the four of us. But when our friend greeted us at the door with her beautiful smile and her melodious southern drawl, she said, "*Bah-bra*, the most unusual thing has happened! We have to go to the Ramada Inn for lunch, because we have more than 450 ladies wanting to meet you!"

"What!" I answered, aghast. The astonished look on my face made her rush on with an explanation. She said her husband had mentioned to his Sunday school class that we were coming . . . and after that the calls quickly came pouring in. The next thing they knew, they were calling the hotel to arrange a banquet-size luncheon!

As we drove up to the hotel, the ladies were lined up around the entrance. In any other situation, what happened next might have been ugly, but these lovely women were so patient it didn't seem to matter that the bookstore, which had quickly set up a table to sell my books, ran out. Nor did anyone get upset when the serving staff ran out of food . . . and eating utensils . . . and chairs. Despite all the shortages—and the big change in plans—we had a terrific time of fellowship and sharing. One lady told me the last "important" person to visit there was Barry Goldwater!

We took a little risk in going there—our schedule was tight, and we were already exhausted as we made that two-hour trip. But what a boost those merry women gave to us. It was a real splash of joy for my memory treasure chest.

Plunging into Public Speaking

One of the risks that quickly grew out of Spatula Ministries was the public speaking appearances. At first it was a little scary to think of standing up in front of an audience and telling my story. The first few times, I was afraid I might forget what I wanted to say . . . that I would cry at the sad parts or that no one would laugh at the funny parts . . . or that someone might be offended by something I said. But I felt God's love pushing me up to the microphone—and the rest was easy. Now I've done it so often I feel confident the Lord will propel the story each time I step up to the podium.

Still, you just never know how accommodating the facility will be or what kind of response an audience will have. At several gatherings in the last couple of years, the facility has been overcrowded and women had to be turned away or shuttled into cramped "overflow" rooms. At one luncheon gathering recently, the church sponsoring the event had ordered box lunches for all the attendees—but there were many more people than they had planned for, and they ran out of food. Being resourceful women, the conference organizers called the city's Rescue Mission, which sent over delicious meals for the two hundred hungry women who hadn't gotten served. There wasn't a single complaint; some women even said the Rescue Mission's lunches were tastier than the catered ones!

My years of public speaking have rewarded me with many blessings. One of them is that I've met *many* very creative women like the ones who found food at the Rescue Mission; for me, this is one of the greatest rewards of undertaking this rather risky adventure. For example, soon after my book *Splashes of Joy in the Cesspools of Life* came out, I was invited to speak at a large banquet at a mega-church in Arizona. As we walked into the banquet room, we were shocked—and delighted—at what we saw.

The room had been decorated "cesspool-style," one of the clever women laughingly told us. Rolls of pink, yellow, blue, and white toilet tissue had been gracefully draped all around the banquet room, and streamers of the tissue formed a wistful curtain to hide the edge of the speakers platform. And *on* the platform were three complete toilets covered with gold paper and sparkly stuff—truly, a sight to behold. Each of the fifty tables was set with a rubber-plunger centerpiece covered with pink feathers, white pearls, and toilet-tissue bows. Can you imagine the fun we had in such a setting?

To start things off, the director of women's ministry stood up and said, "Let's plunge right in, ladies!" Then she taught us a little song: "Flush away, flush away, flush away all," and the place fairly rocked with all the gals laughing, singing, swinging, and swaying.

The crowning joy of the day was the farewell gift the ladies gave us—a lovely toilet seat encrusted with pearls and trimmed with feathers, sprayed all over with more sparklies. Bill hand-carried it all the way back to California, and you can believe he was the talk of the airport that day! Of all the places we've been and all the conferences we've been a part of, THAT was certainly the most memorable decor. It still makes me laugh just to think of it.

After another speaking appearance, we got a splash of joy from a letter written by one of the women attending. She commended the organizers of the Joyful Journey tour, a nationwide series of women's conferences that I participated in. The woman said she appreciated how everything had been planned right down to the smallest detail—even to having Scripture verses taped to the back of the restroom doors! She noted, however, that the Scripture verse she had found in *her* restroom stall had been "a little unsettling." It read, "YOU ARE SURROUNDED BY SO GREAT A CLOUD OF WITNESSES"!

Pots of Thoughtfulness

The women I've met on my travels have not only shared laughter with me, they've also taught me what thoughtfulness is all about. Soon after *Geranium* was published, we were in Canada attending a booksellers convention in August. A local bookstore had invited me to stop by and sign some books while we were there, and I was happy to do it. What a nice surprise to learn, as we arrived, that one of the bookstore employees had started back in March to grow geraniums from seeds in little pots nestled under special lights in her basement—in cold-weathered Canada!

She had lovingly tended eighty of these little seedlings, and by the time I arrived there to sign the books, they were robust and ready for adoption. She generously presented them to me, each little pot wrapped in shiny gold paper, so that I could give them to customers who came to have their books signed. What a treat it was for all of us that day to see those little geraniums going out of the store to spread a bit of joy in someone's window!

Surprises on the Speakers Platform

These are just a few of the ways I've been blessed during all these years of public appearances. Actually, I've been "performing" in front of audiences since I was a young child.

When I accompanied my pastor father to tent revivals around Michigan I was so small I had to stand on a chair to sing "specials" for the gathered congregation. To this day, the smell of wood shavings brings those memories rushing back to my mind.

One of my first performances was as a tiny child wearing a huge, flower-covered hat (visions of things to come, I guess) while singing "Just a little pansy, velvety and brown. On each tiny blossom, God is looking down." Things went well, and I got pretty good at this little number—until the time my mother forgot to STARCH my pansy hat—and the brim flopped pitifully over my eyes. I looked more like a wilted petunia than a perky pansy!

Since then I've rarely felt a moment of stagefright, but I *do* tend to wonder whether something unexpected is going to happen in the middle of my presentation or if I'll commit some inadvertent goof (as I did when I drank the holy water from a baptismal chalice, thinking it was the drinking water I'd requested).

Writing with God's Hand on Mine

The public speaking goes hand-in-hand with another risk I encountered several years ago when, out of the blue, a publisher invited me to write a book about our family's experiences—Bill's devastating accident, the death of two of our sons, and another son's alienation and disappearance. I had just turned FIFTY, and I had never written anything, let alone a book! But the publisher assured me the Lord would propel the book forward, and the result was *Where Does a Mother Go to Resign?* It poured out of me in just eight weeks, and—miracle of miracles—it's still selling well today, eighteen years later, so I know that God's hand was, indeed, guiding mine.

Soon after that project was completed, my friend Lynda sent to a different publisher another manuscript I'd prepared. It had grown out of the journal I'd been keeping throughout the painful years we were struggling to survive. In no time, back came a rather curt letter from the publisher saying my material wasn't suitable for publication. I felt pretty foolish and a little intimidated. Yet I knew God was guiding me, and somehow I continued writing but with more determination to inspire others through my own experiences.

And guess what! The publisher who rejected that proposal was none other than Word, Inc., the wonderful company that's become like a family to me and has published my last five books as well as this one! If ever there was an illustration of "the stone the builders rejected" (Ps. 118:22), I'm it! No one could have been less likely to become an established author than I was when we sent in those pages from my journal all those years ago. And no one could have felt more rejected than I did after that proposal was labeled "unsuitable."

Plenty of other folks were rejected before their efforts succeeded. Author Irvin Stone reportedly collected seventeen rejection letters before a publisher accepted his book *Lust for Life*—which sold twenty-five million copies!

Julia Child's first cookbook was rejected, too, and "Dr. Seuss" got turned down twenty-four times before a publisher finally told him yes.[7]

Abraham Lincoln was defeated in his first run for the Illinois legislature in 1832. Thank goodness he didn't give up politics after that first discouraging failure!

Babe Ruth STRUCK OUT more than thirteen hundred times!

Mother Teresa spent most of her life devotedly working for the poor in Calcutta in relative anonymity. It was only when she was in her seventies that recognition came her way.

Col. Harland Sanders, a seventh-grade dropout, opened his first Kentucky Fried Chicken franchise when he was in his sixties.[8]

Recently I learned that Charles Schulz, the cartoonist who created the "Peanuts" comic strip, was turned down for employment by Walt Disney many years ago because Disney said Schulz's work was just not good enough. Now, there's a star on Hollywood Boulevard with Charles Schulz's name on it. And guess whose star is right next to it: Walt Disney's!

As one editorial writer urged, "Remember that big success is always a possibility, regardless of your age or status. Perseverance is all."[9] Just in case you run out of perseverance before you run into a brick wall on your first attempt at risk-taking, write this verse on an index card and carry it with you wherever you go. Better yet, memorize it, and recite it to yourself regularly:

> [We may be] confident of this, that he who began
> a good work in [us] will carry it on to completion
> until the day of Christ Jesus. (Phil. 1:6)

Retiring Your Retirement

Many retired people are finding innovative ways to "unre-tire." Instead of spending their golden years in "drydock," just waiting for Gabriel to blow his horn, they're going back to work, choosing to be productive instead of consumptive!

You think you're too old to walk into a business and apply for a job? You're not! If that's what you want to do, you're not alone. Millions of Americans over age fifty are taking up new careers, especially in areas that welcome "mature workers."

One article I saw said that banks like to hire older workers because "when customers see dignified tellers . . . they see their money in good hands." Hotels like people in our age bracket because we're dependable. Travel agencies are favorite employers of older people who enjoy traveling and who enjoy the enticing perks of discount hotel rates and airfares.[10]

Furthering God's Kingdom, One Step at a Time

If you just can't bring yourself to take a risk on your own behalf, perhaps it would give you courage to remember that everything you do, you're doing for the Lord. If HE asked you for help, how could you turn Him down?

Well, He's asking! And that doesn't necessarily mean He's asking you to apply to seminary and lead a mission trip to China. There's plenty of work right in your own backyard for those who are willing to do it. Many schools welcome volunteers of all ages. A friend in Florida told me about a gray-haired grandmother who has volunteered at the elementary school in her neighborhood for more than thirty years—long past the time when her own children were students there. In August she calls the school, asking if there are papers to be copied and collated—and there always are. She's been honored several times by that school as one of its otherwise-unheralded "angels."

Another woman didn't even have to venture outside her home to do her good deed. She simply volunteered to be her church's publicity chairman. Every week she typed up a one-paragraph news item describing her church's regular services or special programs that were coming up. She mailed them in to the local newspaper and radio stations to use in their weekly "bulletin board" listings.

Her church was fairly large, with several services during the week, so she never really knew if those little notes that appeared in the paper were effective. Then came the day when the pastor pulled her aside one morning before the service began. He said, "Ann, I'd like you to meet Diane. She and I have met together quite a few times this past month, and she's decided she wants to be a part of our congregation. In fact, she's planning to come forward to be baptized today. And Ann, she started coming to our church because she saw one of the little items you put in the newspaper."

Well, you can imagine how excited Ann was about that news. "I felt almost like a new mother!" she exclaimed. "Diane and I hugged each other, and I'm not sure which one of us was happier."

Volunteers who work with Habitat for Humanity share a similar sense of leading others to Christ in a rather unlikely way. There are hundreds of stories about the lives touched by these home-builders—many of whom are middle-aged women who have never held a hammer in their lives before showing up at a worksite to volunteer. One of my favorite stories is about the Habitat for Humanity work project in Charlotte, North Carolina, that was led by former President

Jimmy Carter in July 1987. In just one week, Carter and his wife, Rosalynn, along with dozens of volunteers, built fourteen houses in a Charlotte neighborhood.

Two years later, Habitat founder Millard Fuller was back in Charlotte and asked a friend to go with him to see the Habitat houses built during the Carter work project. According to Fuller's book *The Excitement Is Building,*

> As they turned around in the cul-de-sac and started driving slowly back up the street, they saw the house Jimmy and Rosalynn Carter had worked on. In the front yard a little boy, maybe six years old, was playing. They stopped the car momentarily, so the boy ran over to greet them.
>
> "Hey," he said, "you got a pretty car."
>
> "Yes, and you have a pretty house. Which one is yours?"
>
> He waved a finger back toward the house.
>
> "What's your name?" Millard asked him.
>
> "D.J."
>
> "Well, D.J., I want to ask you a question. Who built your house?"
>
> Millard thought he would say, "Jimmy Carter." Instead, D.J. quietly replied, "Jesus."[11]

What an honor it would be to have someone feel that Jesus had touched his or her life because of something WE did! Don't let your fears and inertia keep you from reaping these blessings. Remember that God is with you when you venture outside that door.

Someone sent me a little clipping from some unknown source that says,

> The Christian life is a life of faith. . . . I have noticed that God regards faith highly and has a strategy for developing it. He gets us climbing after Him and then when we are committed to the path, He points down and we notice there's no safety net.

God's best moments for us are when we dare all on Him alone, when all our usual ropes and nets have been removed and all we have is Him. "By faith Abraham heard God's call and went . . . even though he didn't know where he was going."

Real faith loves tough situations, for that is where God works most often. Faith laughs at impossibilities and cries, "It shall be done!"

Laugh at Impossibilities

Speaking of Abraham . . . relocating wasn't the only "tough situation" he and his wife, Sarah, risked in their old age. I love the Genesis passage that tells the story of Sarah's risky "adventure," perhaps because Sarah reminds me so much of myself, laughing at the wrong time—and getting caught!

> Then the LORD said [to Abraham], "I will surely return to you about this time next year, and Sarah your wife will have a son."
>
> Now Sarah was listening at the entrance to the tent, which was behind him. Abraham and Sarah were already old and well advanced in years, and Sarah was past the age of childbearing. So Sarah laughed to herself as she thought, "After I am worn out and my master is old, will I now have this pleasure?"
>
> Then the LORD said to Abraham, "Why did Sarah laugh and say, 'Will I really have a child, now that I am old?' Is anything too hard for the LORD? I will return to you at the appointed time next year and Sarah will have a son."
>
> Sarah was afraid, so she lied and said, "I did not laugh."
>
> But he said, "Yes, you did laugh." (Gen. 18:10–15)

Can't you just hear God saying, "Oh yes you did laugh, Sarah!" This old woman may be the only character in the Bible who heard God's voice—and thought He was joking! Thank heaven she didn't do what I would probably want to do if I found out I was pregnant at age ninety—throw myself off a cliff! Instead, Sarah was courageous. And in fact she was delighted by her pregnancy. She seemed to cherish her condition.

When the baby was born Sarah named him Isaac and predicted, "God has brought me laughter, and everyone who hears about this will laugh with me" (Gen. 21:6). She was right; thousands of years later, Sarah's laughter is still contagious.

"...THE ONLY REAL PROBLEM IS I KEEP GETTING HIS 'PAMPERS' MIXED UP WITH MY 'DEPENDS'..."

Reprinted with permission of the *Kansas City Star.*

How Long Since YOU'VE Laughed?

How long has it been since YOU did something outrageous? Maybe not as outrageous as getting pregnant at age ninety . . . but how long has it been since you ate watermelon and tried to see how far you could spit the seeds? Or gathered big armfuls of lilacs and brought them to friends so their homes would smell like spring? Or marched in a parade or climbed *up* the down escalator? Take a chance. Break out of your little plastic mold and become a DINGY person (not din-gee but DING-ee) even if people think you are fresh out of the rubber-room situation.

Did you ever watch a child swat madly at specks of dust hanging suspended in a shaft of sunlight? Children delight at such innocent, simple things—and so can you. Become a child again. Laugh! It's like jogging on the inside. Look for ways to enjoy your day—however small or trivial. Have a joyful atti-tude, the kind that makes you celebrate every good thing that happens, no matter how trivial—even finding a convenient parking space! Look at a field of flowers and see FLOWERS, not WEEDS!

That kind of positive attitude is vividly expressed in these charming Christmas letters from Bruce and Rose Bliven that appeared in Ann Landers's column in 1976 and 1977:

> At 86, Rose and I live by the rules of the elderly:
> If the toothbrush is wet, you have brushed your teeth. If the bedside radio is warm in the morning, you left it on all night. If you are wearing one brown shoe and one black shoe, you have a pair just like it somewhere in the closet.
> Try not to mind when a friend tells you on your birthday that a case of prune juice has been donated in your name to a retirement home.
> I stagger when I walk, and small boys follow me, making bets on which way I'll go next. This upsets me. Children shouldn't gamble.
> Like most elderly people, we spend many happy hours in front of the TV set. We rarely turn it on.

The next year, Ann published this "sequel":

> Dear Friends:
> Rosie and I are now 87. Would we care to try for 174? The answer is no. I'm 46 percent as old as the United States and still can't spell "seize."

Rosie has aged some in the past year and now seems like a woman entering her 40s. She chides me about the little elf who regularly enters our house in the middle of the night, squeezes the toothpaste tube in the middle and departs. Last May, we celebrated our 63rd anniversary.

As for me, I am as bright as can be expected. I remember well the friend who told me years ago, "If your IQ ever breaks 100—sell!"

I walk with a slight straddle, hoping people will think I just got off a horse. On my daily excursions, I greet everyone punctiliously, including the headrests in parked, empty cars. Dignified friends seem surprised when I salute them with a breezy "Hi!" They don't realize I haven't enough breath for a two-syllable greeting.

When we are old, the young are kinder to us and we are kinder to each other. There is a sunset glow that radiates from our faces and is reflected on the faces of those about us. . . .[12]

Wouldn't you love to have friends with a lighthearted attitude like that? The next best thing to having a friend like that who can boost your spirits is to BE A FRIEND who helps others see the laughter in life.

Making a Fresh Start

Does your "sunset glow," like that of Rose and Bruce Blivens, reflect on those about you? Or is your light slowly fading while you huddle at home, feeling sorry for yourself?

As Dr. Samuel Johnson said, "If a man does not make new acquaintances as he advances through life, he will soon find himself left alone." Adds author Sherwood Eliot Wirt, "We seniors should never let pass an opportunity to meet [new friends]." And he insists, "It's a major blunder for us to make friends exclusively among people our own age. If we do that we let the world segregate us!"[13]

© Dana Summers. Reprinted with permission.

Now, it may take some practice to become sociable again. As you overcome your reluctance to reach out to others, you'll have to remember the little adage:

> Hospitality is making your guests feel at home
> even though you wish they were!

In case you're out of practice at making friends, here's a list of excellent tips on how to do that:

Spend time. The best way to get to know someone is to do things you both enjoy together and talk. Look for others who share your interests.

Make eye contact. Looking directly at someone, rather than toward the floor or ceiling, demonstrates your interest in what the person is saying.

Investigate. Ask questions. Discover what someone likes or dislikes. Find out about her job situation, family background, and dreams.

Listen. Interactive conversation shows you care. Learn from the different perspectives others have on issues.

Express esteem. Treat the other person with kindness. Show that you value and respect what he does or thinks.[14]

Did you notice what the first letters of the items in this list spell? SMILE! That's really the first step in reaching out to anyone in friendship.

Cut on dotted line.
Then when you meet someone who needs a smile,
give her one of yours.

Winston Churchill said, "We make a living by what we get. We make a LIFE by what we GIVE." What have you given away to a friend lately?

Have you given someone your smile?

Have you shared your laughter?
How about a hug?
Have you paid someone a compliment lately?
Have you told a friend how special he or she is?
Have you listened with your eyes and your ears?
Have you been there for someone who was hurting?
Did you go out of your way just to be kind?
Were you willing to share your time and your life?[15]

As someone said, "It takes no light away from your own candle to light another." Take a chance! Do something risky. Make a new friend. Do a good deed. Even if you got a late start, it's never too late to do something meaningful with your life!

Do all the good you can by all the means you can in all the ways you can in all the places you can and all the times you can to all the people you can as long as ever you can.

John Wesley

Fill your life with experiences, not excuses.[16]

He who laughs last thinks slowest!

Life is a matter of choice.
You can choose to be thirty years old
or seventy years young.
YOU decide!

Church Bulletin Blunders:
"Don't let worry kill you—let the church help!"
"The ladies of the church have cast off clothing of every kind, and they may be seen in the church basement on Friday."
"The service will close with 'Little Drops of Water.' One of the ladies will start quietly, and the rest of the congregation will join in."

"What does man gain from all his labor at which he toils under the sun?" (Eccles. 1:3)
WRINKLES![17]

As I pulled into the parking lot of a church where I was to speak at an "area-wide women's seminar," I spotted the large, bold sign that had been placed on the church marquee—and HOPED the words had been transposed.
The sign said: WIDE WOMEN'S AREA SEMINAR.

Anything can happen to me tomorrow,
But at least nothing more can happen to me yesterday.

Ashleigh Brilliant
Pot-shot 4374, © 1988

Middle age is when you want to see how long your car will last . . . instead of how fast it will go.

Two sets of grandparents arrived at the hospital together to see their newborn grandson. Just getting out of the car was quite an ordeal since all four were in various stages of recovery from knee operations and hip replacements. As the foursome hobbled toward the hospital entrance, brandishing canes and walkers, one of them quipped, "Mercy! I hope they don't admit us before we get to the maternity ward!"[18]

Suddenly Mine

O Lord
May I believe in the darkness
When all hope has vanished
When waves beat with fury
And no star lights my sky.
May I believe without
Feeling or knowing or proving
Till one shining moment when
You shatter the darkness
And all I believed for
Is suddenly mine.

Ruth Harms Calkin[19]

Classified Ad

For sale: antique desk suitable for lady with thick legs and large drawers.

Then I heard the voice of the LORD saying, "Whom shall I send? And who will go for us?"

And I said, "Here am I. Send me!" (Isa. 6:8)

Precious Memories—
How They Leave Us

Young at heart—
slightly older in other places.

When we are out speaking at seminars and conferences, Bill and I take along several pounds of flat, iridescent marbles about the size of a half-dollar. We give them to the women who visit our book table, telling them the marbles are "splashes of joy" to put on the window sill so that when the sun shines on the shimmering glass, they'll be reminded of God's blessings. It's such fun to give away these smooth, flat sparkles; there's probably more than a ton of them out there in circulation by now!

When the marbles are shipped to me from the manufacturer in small bundles of single colors—red, lilac, blue, amber, purple, and green—they have a powder residue on them. So I have to undo each bundle and place the marbles in the towel-lined kitchen sink and rinse them off. Then I spread them out on a large towel and dry them so they're clean, shining, and lustrous when we hand them out at the book table.

Recently a reporter from some publication called me while I was busy at this task. She said she was calling various authors and other people to find out *precisely* what they were doing at that exact moment.

"Well," I said, wondering how this was going to sound, "I'm washing my marbles in the sink."

She didn't answer for a moment. Then she asked, "Who is this again?"

"It's Barbara Johnson." (I'd already told her that when I first answered the phone.)

"The Christian author?"

"Well, yes, I . . ."

"And you're washing your marbles?"

By this time I'm sure she was wondering if she'd dialed the wrong number and reached the home for the bewildered. Finally she gave me time to explain that I always rinse the splashes of joy we give away at meetings and other gatherings. We had a good laugh about her first reaction. Then I told her that washing my marbles helps me remember how God washes us and cleanses our lives. Our robes of righteousness get caked with grime and grit, and God cleans us. His love washes away all the residue we pick up in life so our robes are white again, clean and shining.

Many of my friends know I love to joke about my marbles— washing them and occasionally *losing* them. In fact, one friend sent me a little plaque that said:

All My Marbles Certificate
This is to certify that I,
Barbara Johnson,
am in possession of All My Marbles.
I can never again be accused of not having All My Marbles.

At the bottom of the certificate, this zany friend had written, "If everyone had All Their Marbles—the world would be a nicer place to live!"

Living in La-La Land

Keeping all our marbles gets harder as we get older, doesn't it? Actually, from our side of our faces, it probably seems that we're still cruising along normally through life, but others notice that we occasionally slip into temporary goofiness—losing our reading glasses when they're on top of our heads, unloading the groceries after a shopping trip and putting the *TV Guide* in the refrigerator and the milk in the closet, forgetting where we parked the car at the mall. These things can happen to anyone, of course, but they seem to happen to us older folks a little more often than to younger people.

This poem sums up the situation perfectly:

> Just a note to send my greetings,
> Let you know I'm still alive,
> Though I'm getting more forgetful.
> Things just seem to slip my mind.
>
> I fuss and fret and try to think,
> But all that comes to me
> Is pain between my eyeballs—
> My head hurts terribly!
>
> I walk into the bathroom
> To retrieve a headache pill.
> There I stand, listing my options,
> Wondering what I'm doing here.
>
> I back into the hallway,
> "Start all over," I suggest.
> Then, remembering what I needed,
> I head back toward the shelf.

But once more, memory fails me.
"Why am I here?" I ask.
Then my eye falls on my toothbrush,
And I take my dentures out.

Still, it seems like there was something else . .
"What could it be?" I pose.
Then I fill the tub with water
And sit down awhile to soak.

"This isn't it," I tell myself.
"I came for something more."
Then I spy the scales and, dripping wet,
Stride quickly 'cross the floor.

I step onto the circular disk
And struggle hard to see
The numbers on the dial below—
"Where could my glasses be?"

I step into the bedroom,
Where I'm sure my specs I'll find.
But standing there beside the bed,
I just cannot decide

Why I've come there—did the phone ring?
Then I see the looking glass.
Good heavens! I'm stark naked!
I'd better get dressed—fast!

I step up to the closet,
Pull the chain to flick the light.
My nightgown hangs before me.
"Oh! It's time to say good night."

I slip into my nightie
As I hum a sleep-tight song,

Pull the covers up around me—
But wait! There's something wrong.

It's the sun. It's at my window!
How could day arrive so soon?
Then I spy the clock and blink my eyes.
"For heaven's sake! It's noon!"

I hurry to the bathroom,
Since I'm running far behind.
There I stand, listing my options,
Wondering what I came to find.

I see this note I started—
Now I can't remember when.
"I'll finish it, right now, right here—
If I can find a pen."

I shuffle to the kitchen,
Where by chance I come upon
A recipe for turnips.
But, my stars! The type is small.

I squint and try to read it,
But my focus is so bad,
A pain streaks o'er my temples—
Creates misery in my head.

I walk into the bathroom
To retrieve a simple pill . . .
It all seems so familiar—
What AM I doing here?

                    Ann Luna

   One of the biggest problems we have with forgetfulness is
forgetting what we've already said. We repeat ourselves—
but, after all, that's one of the prerogatives of aging, isn't it? I

saw a little cartoon with an old man saying to a friend, "At my age, I realize I've already said everything I ever wanted to say, so from here on out, I'll just be repeating myself."

The danger, of course, is that some of us think we really do know EVERYTHING when we've gained a little seniority over the rest of the world. As somebody said:

I KNOW IT ALL.
I JUST CAN'T REMEMBER IT ALL AT ONCE!

Memory Mischief

For some of us, the biggest challenge of our advancing years is not remembering names, faces, and events that occurred decades ago. It's remembering what happened a couple of hours ago. With each footstep we take into the future, some of us loosen our grip on our SHORT-TERM memory. To put it bluntly, we can't remember what we just said.

And another problem we have is that we can't remember what we just said! (Just kidding!)

Have you seen the glaze slide over someone's eyes when you start in on a story about some exciting adventure you've had? Some bargain you found? Some delicious feast you enjoyed? Sure you've seen it—it's the disengaging message that says, *I've already heard this story two dozen times.* If only we could REMEMBER what that eye-glaze means when we see it, but no! We just keep prattling away, laying out all the little details about who said what and who did this and—

Now what was I talking about? Oh yes, remembering what we just said. Well, the important thing is, if we're going to repeat our stories endlessly, we owe it to our friends and relatives to at least make the stories HAVE A POINT and, even better, BE ENTERTAINING.

This is a real challenge for some of us, because we start off in one direction and remember something even more earth-shaking. As Ravi Zacharias said, quoting an unknown sage, "Old age is signaled when everything you hear reminds you of something else."[1] You start off on a tale about your cruise down the Mississippi, and before you know it, you're giving your shoe size and the recipe for baked apples, but . . . now, where was I going with this? Oh yes, making our stories interesting and STAYING ON TRACK!

Well, my only REAL advice on this topic is to hang on to your sense of humor as you lose your grip on reality.

Someone sent me a little piece of advice that said, "What I know from having lived a long life is . . . a sense of humor helps. Memory helps. You can get by with one or the other, but when you lose both, you're vegetation."[2]

A friend wrote me a wonderful letter that said:

> Since I've become a grandmother, I guess I'm in the golden years. I try to keep an upbeat attitude and laugh a lot. Sometimes I don't remember what I'm laughing about, but it must have been funny, so I keep on.
>
> It seems memory loss is a big factor in growing older. The neat thing is that my friends are all in the same boat, so their feelings won't be hurt when I forget because they don't remember either! If I do something stupid, I won't remember long enough to stay embarrassed.

Mental Aerobics

Experts say one of the best ways to hang on to your memory is to exercise your mind. That doesn't mean you have to learn a new language or try to memorize the names of everyone in the House of Representatives. It just means "staying mentally active."

And how do you do that? Memorizing beautiful Scripture verses is one of the best ways. Being able to repeat those soothing, comforting messages is not only good mental experience, it's good for our souls as well! In times of trouble, it can be a lifeline back to sanity.

One expert suggests "reading and participating in such challenging activities as carpentry, piano-playing and games like chess [or] backgammon. . . . Some studies show that bridge players have better memories than non-bridge players. Others suggest that doing anagrams and crossword puzzles may amount to mental maintenance. Favor the complex over the simple, the active over the passive. Chess is better for your brain than checkers. But checkers is better than watching television."[3] Here are some other tricks for jump-starting your memory:

- **Get all the gadgets.** Beepers, computers, and electronic daily planners can remind you to take your medicine or mow the lawn. . . . So go ahead, get one of those key rings that chirps when you clap your hands.

- **Make notes.** Rather than write a list you could forget to look at, try putting Post-It notes in places where you can't possibly miss them. If you have to call your daughter in the morning, post a note on something you use every morning—like the coffeepot or shower head.

- **Block the doorway.** If you need to return *Now, Voyager* to the video store, don't put it on the kitchen counter where you'll forget it. Drop it on the floor, right in front of the door.

- **Create memory prods.** Remember how the sentence Every Good Boy Does Fine helped you recall the treble notes (E,G,B,D,F) in music class? Use this technique with a shopping list. If you need lettuce, sugar, napkins, chicken, rice, and soup, keep in mind that Little Serpents Never Climb Rickety Stairs. If you come up with an odd enough visual image, you'll be surprised how often you'll remember it.

- **Rely on state-dependent recall.** Remember when you marched into the kitchen, a [woman] on a mission, only to arrive there and forget what the mission was? Well, sit back down in the La-Z-Boy whence you came. Studies indicate that returning to the state you were in when you had the thought often gives your memory just the jump start it needs.

- **When in doubt, stall.** Many memory problems are momentary. So, . . . buy yourself a moment. How?

Take a sip of coffee. Cough and feign a frog in your
throat. You might even stop mid-sentence and compliment someone in the room about his necktie.
Many times, a few extra seconds is all you need to
come up with an elusive name.[4]

This last tip reminds me of a darling little white-haired
lady I met last year at a retreat in Texas. Her eyes always had
a merry twinkle, and the smile never left her face. She wasn't
at all perturbed at her own occasional memory lapses. At one
point someone asked her a question, and she paused, blinked
a few times, and raised an index finger to her lips in an effort
to remember the answer. Finally, she said:

"Do you need to know right now,
or could you wait a little while?"

This lady may have had a slow memory, but she more than
compensated for it by exhibiting a wonderfully quick wit.
Little zingers like that help the people around us realize that
the QUALITY of our minds (for the most part, at least!) is as
good as ever. It just takes us a little longer to kick-start our
brains into action!

We've all struggled to put a name with a face that seems so
familiar. Other times the NAME is familiar, but the face is a
mystery. That kind of situation brought a laugh to us recently
when I was speaking at a women's retreat and a beautiful
African American woman came up to me after lunch. She had
the brightest, widest smile that flashed from her dark face,
and her shiny black hair was carefully braided into dozens of
tiny braids that swung merrily as she walked.

With a mischievous giggle, she pointed to her nametag
and laughed about the fact that her name was BARBARA
JOHNSON too. She said, "Barbara, when I came through the
lunch line, they saw my nametag and thought I was you.
They gave me my lunch for free!"

Slow Memory, Quick Wit

One of the good things about modern technology is all the wonderful little gadgets that have been developed to help us deal with the challenges of aging. One of the best gifts I've ever received is a tiny little gadget on a keyring that I can speak into to record thirty-second reminder messages to myself. My friends Marilyn Meberg and Pat Wenger bought it for me so when I park my car at the mall, I can just raise the keyring to my lips and say, "Row E, space 12," and later, when I'm out on the pavement, wondering where on earth my car is, my little keyring will tell me exactly where it is (IF I CAN JUST REMEMBER TO PRESS THE BUTTON!).

"I'm always losing my car keys, my temper, my memory and my patience... so losing weight should be a breeze!"

It's a wonderful aid for those times when it's close to suppertime and Bill's not home and I have that sneaky feeling I've forgotten something. When I push the button, I hear my own voice reminding me, "Don't forget to pick up Bill at the car-repair place at 5:30!"

My friends got me this great little gadget because we've spent a lot of time together during the last year as part of the Joyful Journey tour. Being in many airports and changing planes and schedules, they have seen me jot down on my hand the flight number or the phone number for whoever is picking me up. Truly this little device has been a godsend for me. It's like having a second mind! Now I can wash my hand without erasing all my important notes!

Reliving the Good Times

Another way to exercise our memories—if we don't overdo it and get STUCK in the past—is to reminisce. Recall happy memories as often as you wish; they never wear out. Experts say remembering beloved memories helps us preserve our identities and maintain our self-esteem.

We joke that our memories deteriorate as we age, but the truth is that unless we're afflicted with TOTAL memory loss due to Alzheimer's or dementia, our brains serve as amazing libraries of information for us. One writer suggests that we use the incredible gift of memories for pleasure—as a means of soothing and comforting ourselves. She writes:

> Even if you regularly lose your keys, forget where you parked your car, or misplace important papers, your memory stores more information than all the libraries in the world. Your brain is far more sophisticated than any computer. You may have forgotten an incident, and then twenty years later something cues that memory—a smell, a sound, a person, a picture—and instantly your mind recalls massive details about an event.
>
> Think of how many voices you recognize on the telephone. One time, a friend whom I hadn't talked to in twenty years called me. All he said was "Hello," and before he said his name I knew who it was. . . .
>
> Someone starts reciting a nursery rhyme or a story you knew as a child, and it all comes back.

Another way to marvel at your amazing memory is to pull out old photos. As you look at them, notice how images burst upon your conscious mind. . . .

Reminisce with people about past times. Before I moved from Minnesota, one of the most healing ways to ease the separation . . . was to talk about turning points, the ways people had been helpful to each other, the times someone had been mad or wanted to leave. Often someone would say, "Oh, I had forgotten that." We ended up laughing, crying, and appreciating the richness of our experience together—as if everyone had brought an ingredient for a cake and we put it all together. And somehow, with all the memories more alive in our minds, it was easier to part because we knew the memories would stay with us.[5]

Sharing Special Memories

Memory is a form of immortality. Those we remember never die; they continue to walk and talk with us, and their influence is with us as long as we remember them. Shared memories can also be a bridge that brings us to new acquaintances. That's what happened for us recently when I was speaking at a women's conference in Boston.

A darling gal came up to me, obviously thrilled about something. I could hardly wait to find out what it was. She excitedly told me that she had lived in Anchorage, Alaska, several years ago, and now she lived in Boston. She had never read any of my books or heard anything about me, but she had decided to come to the women's conference.

During my presentation, I told the audience about the car crash many years ago in a remote part of Canada that had killed our son Tim and his friend Ron as they were driving back after spending several months in Alaska. Tim had called me just a few hours before he was killed; he'd told me he had undergone a spiritual rebirth, that he'd come to know the Lord in a new and invigorating way, and that he couldn't wait to get home and tell me all about it. The next long-distance phone call I received was from the Royal Canadian Mounted Police, telling me both boys had been killed by a drunk driver. As I described to the audience how our family struggled through this heartbreaking time, I held up a picture of Tim's smiling face.

That's when this darling gal realized *she had known Tim in Alaska!* In fact, she had been at the prayer meeting he attended the night before he left Anchorage to drive back home to California. She had been part of the group that had prayed for him and shared the excitement he'd felt about returning home to share his new-found joy with his family.

The young lady said when I'd held up his picture and she saw Tim's face, "everything fell into place." Suddenly she remembered sitting there with Tim, singing and raising their hands in praise, Tim's leaving with excitement and joy, anticipating the journey back to California, obviously with his new relationship with the Lord. The girl was overjoyed to be able to share this memory with me; suddenly, she said, it was as if it all had happened yesterday instead of more than twenty years ago.

What a bittersweet moment that was for us both, and how refreshing it was for me to see her joy in sharing this memory with someone (me!) for whom it meant so much. Later she even sent me photographs of that prayer meeting, and once again, I see my son's smiling face in the midst of a group of enthusiastic young folks.

Truly, memory is a mental bank account. In it we deposit the treasures of our lives so that, in time of need, we can withdraw hope and courage. These treasures are memories large and small: splashes of joy ranging from a pat on the back, the beauty of a full moon on a special evening, finding an empty parking space when we were in a terrible rush, enjoying a glorious sunset with someone we love. Remembering all these happy memories can make us feel like mental millionaires!

Laughter in the Cemetery

For Tim and me, one special memory was feasting on fast food from the In-n-Out Hamburger stand. We would often stop there when he was learning how to drive. Bill was recovering from the devastating effects of an accident[6] at that time, so the driver's training was left up to me. During those weeks I sure learned the truth of the little ditty that says:

> My nerves are a-twitter; my hair has gone white.
> My knees, they are knocking; I'm quaking with fright.
> My whole life is streaking in front of my eyes.
> "Dear Lord, please be with me!" I urgently cry.
> My heart's in my throat, but at least I'm alive.
> The problem? I'm teaching my son how to drive!

It may seem strange to those who've never tried to find a quiet, safe place in the city where a kid can learn how to drive without fighting rush-hour traffic and multi-lane freeways, but Tim and I chose a nearby cemetery. It was beautiful and peaceful, and my favorite part was that the speed limit was only fifteen miles per hour! We would drive around the beautiful grounds for a while, then we'd head for In-n-Out, where I would recover from the experience while Tim stuffed himself with burgers and fries. Then we would go back to the cemetery and try negotiating all the curves again.

It seems like only yesterday that we spent those lovely afternoons together. As Psalm 90:4 puts it:

> For a thousand years in thy sight are but as yesterday when it is past, and as a watch in the night. (KJV)

Someone has said, "Yesterday is a secret room in your heart where you keep the memories of other years." In this secret room we cherish the laughter from another time and again hear the melodies of half-forgotten songs. Today is filled with hurried hustle-bustle, and tomorrow is a mystery, but our yesterdays are treasures from the past to be cherished and enjoyed again and again. There's a lovely little verse that says:

> The heart is like a treasure chest that's filled with souvenirs;
> It's where we keep the memories we've gathered through the years.

Years have passed since Tim and I slowly wound our way through that beautiful cemetery around and around as he learned to drive. Now Tim's grave is right there next to the curving road where we drove together. Recently I was there, standing beside his grave, remembering how we laughed as we rode along that cemetery trail, enjoying the day together.

While I was reliving those bittersweet memories, I could see a little car wending its way along that same path where Tim and I had been so many years ago. In the passenger seat was a young mother, probably about thirty-five, and steering the car I could see a nervous young boy who must have been about fifteen. As the car was coming closer to where I was standing, I wanted to call out to that mother, "Enjoy your ride with him now, while you can. Make a memory of your experience—and go get a hamburger to celebrate!"

Before I knew it, my heart was smiling and a great feeling of peace flowed through me. I was thankful for that bittersweet memory of long ago.

The Tapestry of Our Lives

Reminiscing helps us put our lives into perspective. As we get older, we can see how each stage, every memory, fits into the grander scheme of things. My life has included sorrow as well as happiness. And all those emotions, all those bittersweet memories, have created what I like to think of as a bright, colorful, firmly woven tapestry.

The happy times are the golden threads that catch the sunlight, warming the soul. The bright pattern was created by our children and then the grandchildren, whose sparkling threads added a nubby texture, a splash of vivid color, to the fabric. The black, somber woof threads that subdue the tapestry's gaudiness were painstakingly woven as we endured hardships in life.

Some of the threads in my tapestry are frayed. Others are broken. But the tapestry remains intact because other threads, as invisible as love yet as strong as the everlasting arms, are woven amongst the weakened ones, holding the delicate fibers together.

As I reminisce, I think of how we wove our way through joys and sorrow, good times and bad, glorying in each other's triumphs and supporting each other in times of trial. And in every loop and knot of our lives together, I see the hand of God.

AGE is mostly a matter of mind.
If you don't mind it, it doesn't matter. [7]

TODAY'S FORECAST: Partly rational with brief periods of coherent thought giving way to complete apathy by tonight.[8]

What goes around, comes around . . . and will whack you on the back of the head when it does.[9]

GOOD NEWS: I've finally discovered the Fountain of Youth.

BAD NEWS: At my age, I've forgotten what I wanted to do with it.[10]

The only good thing about the decline of my memory is that it has brought me closer to my mother, for she and I now forget everything at the same time.[11]

I'm not confused, I'm just well-mixed.

Robert Frost

Never ask old people how they are if you have anything else to do that day.

Joe Restivo

Menopause is a mother's revenge for all the times you tried her patience after age fifty.[12]

My mind not only wanders,
sometimes it leaves completely.

One of the side benefits of forgetting names and faces:
You keep meeting new people every day![13]

A little old lady had to go to a gynecologist. Her husband took her to the doctor's office and waited in the waiting room.

When the old lady was settled in the examining room, the doctor asked, "Are you sexually active?"

"Just a minute," the woman replied, looking rather confused and starting to head for the door. "I'll ask my husband."

"No, no," said the doctor. "Let me put it another way. Do you and your husband still have intercourse?"

"I'll ask my husband," the woman said, jumping up from her chair and heading down the hall. She opened the door into the waiting room and hollered, "George, do we still have intercourse?"

Her husband snorted in exasperation and hollered back, "How many times do I have to tell you, Martha? We still have BLUE CROSS!"

It's no use having a good memory,
Unless you have something good to remember.

Ashleigh Brilliant
Pot-shot 3227, © 1985

Hello, welcome to the Psychiatric Hotline.

If you are obsessive-compulsive, please press 1 repeatedly.

If you are co-dependent, please ask someone to press 2.

If you have multiple personalities, please press 3, 4, 5, and 6.

If you are paranoid-delusional, don't do any-thing. We know who you are and what you want. Just stay on the line until we can trace the call.

If you are schizophrenic, listen carefully and a little voice will tell you which number to press.

If you are depressive, it doesn't matter which number you press. No one will reply, and nothing will really ever change anyway.

If you have an Oedipus complex, have your mother help you press two.

If you have attention deficit disorder, we can't help you because you have probably already hung up by now.[14]

Behold, thou desirest truth in the inward parts: and in the hidden part thou shalt make me to know wisdom. (Ps. 51:6 KJV)

Grandmothers Are Antique Little Girls

Grandkids are God's reward for our having survived parenthood!

The day I first felt old is burned like a bittersweet image that haunts my memory. We were visiting with our youngest son, Barney, and his adorable wife, Shannon—and enjoying the cute antics of our precious granddaughter, Kandee. As she played with the new toy we had brought her, little Kandee, who had just celebrated her first birthday, suddenly looked up and flashed her two-tooth smile at Barney. She toddled over and grabbed his knee, excitedly patting it and proclaiming, "Daaah! Daah! Daaah-DEEE!"

That was the moment when old age settled on my doorstep—when this wonderful little creature called my youngest son "Daddy."

It just didn't seem possible. After all, Barney was the

youngest of our four boys, the one I'd brought home from the hospital in a bright red Christmas stocking just a few short years ago—or at least it *seemed* like a few short years. Somehow it had been easy to accept his getting married and moving out of the house. In fact, having him out on his own had given Bill and me a new sense of freedom for the many opportunities that awaited us in the years ahead.

Sure, there were a few moments of mixed feelings later when Barney and Shannon told us we were about to become grandparents. We were joyous, of course, but there was just a momentary pause in our celebration as we considered the new titles we were about to acquire. When Kandee was born, however, any hesitation was forgotten as we snuggled her in our arms and practiced up on forgotten baby-talk.

But now here she was, a toddler, moving on her own and obviously starting to think on her own. AND SHE WAS CALLING *MY SON* "DADDY"! Yes, at that moment I felt old.

Now, each of us responds differently about being a grandmother. One writer said:

> I wanted to be a grandmother, and I was teetering between senility and death. My interest span was becoming limited, patience was in short supply, and I was beginning to forget all the cute games and nursery rhymes. . . . In a few years, I'd throw the baby up into the air and forget to catch him. . . . I wanted people to stop me in a supermarket and say, "Your baby is beautiful!" and I would fan myself with a pound of bacon and protest, "Oh, puleeese, I'm the grandmother."[1]

Wouldn't that be wonderful, to be mistaken for our grandchildren's parents? It's so much better that way than when the opposite occurs. My friend Sue had that horrifying experience when she had just turned thirty and had given birth to a darling baby girl.

On her first solitary trip out of the house after the baby was born, she admittedly looked a little frumpy—prematurely way, she was still carrying a few extra pounds and had been so rushed to put on any makeup. She hurried into a baby boutique to buy something frilly for her daughter. She picked out a beautiful little dress and took it to the counter.

"Oh, isn't this sweet!" exclaimed the saleswoman. "Are you buying this for your GRANDBABY?"

Sue said she was so shocked she called her husband and told him she would be a little late getting home. Then she drove directly to the beauty shop in tears, burst in the door, and wailed, "This is an emergency! This gray hair has got to go!"

THE FAMILY CIRCUS   By Bil Keane

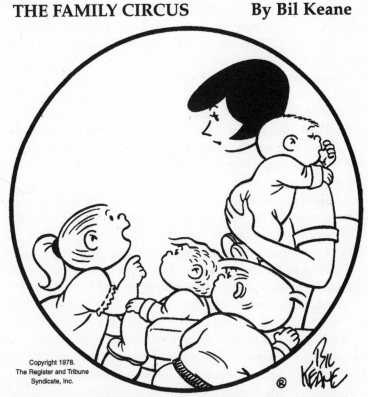

Copyright 1978.
The Register and Tribune
Syndicate, Inc.

"Mommy, when you get old how many grandchildren are you gonna have?"

Forgotten Joys

As someone said, grandchildren "give us pause on the way to heaven." With their arrival, they bring a rush of emotions that sweep over us, temporarily detouring us off the aging track. As soon as we get over the shock of being called "Grandma" many of us find ourselves consumed with new, youthful energies and interests we never would have dreamed we'd have: watching cloud formations change or throwing pebbles into ponds or watching squirrels frolic in the treetops.

We look in those little faces and see a miraculous blending of generations and genes: a grandfather's cheekbones, a mother's eyes, a sibling's dimples. And that fresh new face composed of familiar parts reminds us of loved ones living and gone and of all the emotions and history we've shared with them.

Grandchildren are truly a joy!

BUT . . .

They're also exhausting.

And they (and their parents!) can be quite demanding.

And sometimes they live too far away to visit often.

And sometimes they live too close to give us any privacy or "time off."

And sometimes our other responsibilities or problems—continuing careers, our own needy parents, or strained relationships—can make grandparenting a very trying situation.

Whatever our situations are, we must pray for patience—and strive to be the best grandparents we can be, modeling Christlike love to our grandchildren at every opportunity.

Max Lucado wasn't talking specifically about grandparenting when he wrote the following encouragement for those who "want to make a difference in the world," but it's easy to see how living this kind of "holy life" could be a powerful example for the little ones who might be watching us. He wrote:

> You want to make a difference in your world?
> Live a holy life.

Be faithful to your spouse. Be the one . . . who
refuses to cheat. Be the neighbor who acts neigh-
borly. Be the employee who works and doesn't
complain. Pay your bills. Do your part and enjoy
life. Don't speak one message and live another.

Note Paul's words in 1 Thessalonians 4:11–12:
"Do all you can to lead a peaceful life. Take care of
your own business, and do your own work as we
have already told you. If you do, then people who
are not believers will respect you."

A peaceful life leads nonbelievers to respect
believers. If John the Baptist's life had not matched
his words, his message would have fallen on deaf
ears.

So will ours. People are watching the way we act
more than they are listening to what we say.[2]

Children are especially prone to "watch the way we act
more than they listen to what we say." What a gift we give
them when we show them this kind of role model. Many
children these days have two working parents and a
lifestyle that's always in a rush. Each day they may be hurriedly shuffled from home to school to soccer practice (or
dance class) to daycare to supper to homework to bed.
Whew! And to think that many of them have this schedule
all their lives!

A Haven in Grandmother's Garden

Think of the haven we provide these grandchildren when
we invite them to share a peaceful, unhurried afternoon at the
zoo or "working" in our gardens or looking for butterflies in
the park. To make them the center of attention for even a brief
while lets them know—more than mere words could do—
how much we cherish them.

Imagine what it's like for a little one to be held in a grandmother's arms and hear her lovingly pray, "Thank You, God,
for this dear child, for the joy he brings me and the pride I

have in him! Thank You for giving me such a wonderful gift to cherish!"

Of course, merely imagining such a scene doesn't do much good. Instead, try your best to DO IT whenever you can!

Supergrannies

Indeed, many grandmothers these days struggle with the same time pressures as the grandchildren and their parents are coping with. Most of us grew up with the stereotypical image of a grandmother as that cute little woman with her white hair pulled up into a bun, wearing an apron while she sits in her rocking chair, peeling apples to put in a homemade pie, but that image is probably much more accurate in depicting OUR grandmothers than in describing our grandkids' grandmothers (us!).

Someone sent me a little clipping from an unidentified source that comes closer to describing many grandmothers today. It says, "Move over, Superwoman. Here comes Supergranny, that fifty-plus ball of fire who has a pilot's license, a law degree, and a doctorate in political science!"

It's true. Many women sail through the half-century mark on their way up the corporate ladder—or Mount Everest. Astronaut Shannon Lucid isn't the only gray-haired woman who's setting records and making stunning achievements in what used to be called middle age (or even OLD age!). I think this little poem sums it up pretty well:

Supergranny

Don't look for her in the rocking chair,
Granny isn't in it.
She's off to fight a fire somewhere
Or serving in the Senate.

She might be in a cockpit
Or removing an appendix,
Or checking test tubes in a lab
Or speaking from a pulpit.

She could be on a book tour
Or working as a chef.
Or running a big company
From behind a corporate desk.

A lot has changed in granny's world;
She studies to keep up.
But one thing still comes naturally:
That special Granny LOVE!

Ann Luna

Grandmother Show-and-Tell

Just imagine what it's like these days in grade-school class-rooms on Grandparents Day as the proud students introduce

© 1987 by Mary McBride. Repritned from *Grandma Knows Best, But No One Ever Listens!* with permission of Meadowbrook Press, Minnetonka, MN.

their guests. Can't you just hear the students saying, "My grandmother is a banker," or "My grandmother is a doctor," or "My grandmother is a professor"? The most amazing introductions—and they're surely coming—will be, "My grandmother is PRESIDENT!" or "My grandma is a TRAPEZE ARTIST!"

Actually, while these titles would surely impress the adults in the room, they probably wouldn't mean all that much to the kids. In front of their classmates, they might like to brag that their grandmothers are airline pilots or firefighters, but in all probability that's NOT the thing they care most about. The important thing to most young grandchildren is not TITLES but TIME. That seems to be the sentiment in the following essay. I don't know who wrote it, but she obviously had a wonderful grandmother.

What Is a Grandmother?

A grandmother is a lady who has no children of her own. She likes other people's little boys and girls. A grandfather is a man grandmother. He goes for walks with the boys and they talk about fishing and tractors and stuff like that.

Grandmothers don't have to do anything but be there. They are old, so they shouldn't play hard or run. Instead they drive us to the market where the mechanical horse is and have lots of dimes ready. Or they take us for walks, and they slow down past things like pretty leaves and caterpillars. They never say "Hurry up."

Usually grandmothers are fat, but not too fat to tie your shoes. They wear glasses and funny underwear. They can take their teeth and gums off.

It is better if grandmothers don't typewrite or play cards, except with us. They don't have to be smart, only answer questions like, "Why do dogs chase cats?" or "How come God isn't married?"

Grandmothers don't talk baby talk like strangers

do because it's hard to understand. When they read to us they don't try to skip pages, and they don't mind if it's the same story over again.

Everybody should try to have a grandmother, especially if you don't have TV, because they are the only grown-ups who have time.

Kids have a knack for getting right to the heart of things, don't they? That reminds me of the story I heard about a little boy who was being cared for by his grandma. The little boy had lots of questions, which his grandmother tried patiently to answer. But when he asked, "How old are you?" she replied, "Honey, you're not supposed to ask ladies their age."

Then he said, "Well, how much do you weigh?" to which she gently replied with the same answer.

Then he said, "How come you and Grandpa got a divorce?"

Finally becoming exasperated, she said, "That's nothing for you to be concerned about. Now, go out and play."

Later in the day, the little boy found his grandmother's purse. He dug through it, looking for candy, and instead found her wallet, including her driver's license. Excitedly, the little boy ran to his grandmother and said, "Grandma, I know how old you are and I know how much you weigh . . . and I even know how come you and Grandpa got a divorce!"

She asked him how he could possibly know that, and he answered proudly, "You got a divorce because you got an F in SEX!"

Holiday Hilarity

One of the most important roles we grandparents play is sitting in the audience, watching from the grandstand, and leading every round of applause when our grandchildren are performing somewhere, whether it's horse shows, debate tournaments, or gymnastics meets. Kids love to have us there —so we ought to try to stay awake and act interested!

Some of the funniest stories I've ever heard describe children's antics in Christmas pageants. Of course, at the time they may not be quite so funny—but a few years later they're the highlight of any family gathering.

One of our family's favorite stories is about Larry, our lighthearted son, who was always looking for a little mischief. One year when he was scheduled to appear in our church's Christmas program to sing "As Shepherds Watched Their Flocks by Night," he jokingly "practiced" for weeks at home, singing, "As shepherds washed their socks at night."

The whole family was in stitches every time he broke into that chorus; in fact, at one point, I offered him five dollars if he would get up in front of the church and, like Frank Sinatra, do it "his way." (I guess I've always been one who's perpetually looking for a little mischief too!)

Well, he acted horrified that I even suggested it—and accused me of bribing him to "commit a crime." On the night of the Christmas program, his stomach was full of butterflies, and his little heart was racing because he was so nervous. He shakily stepped up to his "spot" on the platform, took a big breath, and—you guessed it—unintentionally burst out with, "As shepherds washed their socks at night"!

That was the most memorable Christmas program for our family. But we weren't alone in having some unintentional holiday gaffs. Someone gave me this little collection of Christmas-pageant antics, and I enjoy them all over again every time I read them:

- A few days before Christmas I walked into the room where my small son was playing, just in time to hear him singing, "Ho-ly infant, so tenderfoot ride . . ."

- While the art class was setting up a Christmas scene on the school lawn, one of the boys asked uncertainly, "Where do we put the three wise guys?"

- Then there were the four youngsters in the Christmas pageant each carrying a letter to form the word "S-T-A-R," but they went up in reverse order, accidentally spelling "R-A-T-S."

- After the Sunday school class had sung "Silent Night" and had been told the Christmas story, the teacher suggested they draw the nativity scene. A little boy finished first. The teacher praised his drawing of the manger, of Joseph, of Mary, and the infant Jesus. But she was puzzled by a roly-poly figure off to one side. "Who is this?" she asked.

  "Oh, that's Round John Virgin," the little boy replied.

Antique Grandmothers

A friend told me about some grandparents who were showing their little grandson an antique fire engine. The grandfather explained to the little guy that "antique" meant the fire engine was OLD. The boy thought about it a moment then asked, "So are YOU a GRANTIQUE?"

Isn't that a great title? Sort of spiffs us up and puts a higher "market value" on some of us, don't you think? It's certainly pleasanter to think of ourselves as "grantiques" rather than OLD! And anyway, some of the things sold as antiques these days really are quite young. It's amazing to go into antique shops and see things we used only a few years ago (at least it SEEMS like just a few years ago) being sold as highly collectible treasures!

A little news item recently announced the rather surprising age of a product many of us wish we had had when we were new mothers: disposable diapers. The article said Pampers turned thirty-five years old last year, having been invented in 1956. Ironically the inventor was a MAN who came up with the idea while he was babysitting his granddaughter and "was introduced to the joys of changing and washing diapers."[3]

Special Times with Grandma

Grandparenting is probably the most fun when the grandkids are little, when some of the best times we can have come by DOING things with the little ones. Una McManus shared several good ideas in "Grandma, Let's Play," an article she wrote for *A Better Tomorrow* magazine. Some of her suggestions are:

- **Write love letters.** As soon as a grandchild is born, write letters to him or her regularly. . . . Tell your grandchild about himself, his birth, and his development. . . . Store the letters in an attractive box until the child is old enough to appreciate them. . . . [Then] bind your letters into a "love book."

- **Keep a "little things" drawer.** During their early years, your grandchildren will love to have a drawer of their own in your home. Fill it with little things you collect for them, such as free soaps, toys from cereal boxes, sample jellies, free novelty pencils, homemade crafts, and small souvenirs or postcards from trips.

- **Create homemade cards together.** When a grandchild comes to visit, sit down together at the kitchen table and make a list of family birthdays, anniversaries, graduations, and other celebrations. Then get out construction paper, crayons, old magazines and cards, . . . glue, and scissors and go to work making homemade greeting cards. . . .

- **Share a photo memory.** Develop extra copies of photographs and make reprints of old snapshots. Then create a family photo album for each grandchild. . . . Take an evening or a Sunday afternoon to go through the album with the child. Use each photo as a springboard for sharing thoughts about the person and the place. . . .

- **Decorate pancakes.** When grandkids spend the night, make breakfast fun in the morning by creating "funny face pancakes" together. Raisins, cherries, cake decorations, and pieces of cut-up fruit can serve as eyebrows, mouths, and noses. . . . Let the child pour, decorate, and taste to his heart's content. . . .

- **Teach a skill.** . . . Perhaps you can take lessons with your grandchildren to learn something new for both of you such as skiing, calligraphy, or puppet making. . . .

- **Create a "Grandparents' Week" tradition.** Invite the grandchildren for a week during the summer and devote that week to their interests.[4]

The Adolescent Years

While the younger years may be the most fun, many grandmothers enjoy an even more meaningful relationship with their grandchildren as they reach adolescence and the teenage years. These are the times when children typically tend to rebel against parents and expectations. So they often turn for solace during these turbulent times to their grandparents, especially if the elders have shown them unconditional love during the children's growing-up years.

Recently I heard someone reminisce, saying that as a teenager he had fled many times to his grandmother's kitchen after an argument with his parents. There he had found unquestioning acceptance.

"She never asked a lot of questions," the young man said. "She didn't take sides. She really didn't talk much at all. She just opened her door—and her heart—and took me in. Maybe part of the relief I felt by being with her was that my parents had always expected so much of me—and Grandmother expected NOTHING of me, except that I let her love me."

This grandmother had probably never read any of the self-help books that are out there these days, offering wise advice on how to reach out to teens when they're going through family crises. But she showed great wisdom in opening her heart and especially by LISTENING nonjudgmentally.

One expert recommends a twelve-word limit for parents (and it would surely work for grandparents too) during conversations with their kids. The article said, "Teens are all too accustomed to parents' rapid-fire interrogation and long dissertations about the mistakes their kids are making. . . . Keep your comments to your kids (including adult children) to twelve words at a time—or fewer. The same holds true for answers to their questions. It prevents your children from tuning out what you're saying, as well as increases their curiosity, and that raises more questions from them. Because you're responding to their inquiries (not the other way around, as usual), you won't wear them down with too much talk and you'll actually listen better."[5]

Grandma's Love Bank

Being a grandparent doesn't mean we're old, of course. In fact, there are a lot of grandmothers out there who haven't even hit forty yet! But being a grandmother DOES mean we have a special opportunity. We can be a source of unfailing, unquestioning, nonjudgmental, nonstop, full-powered love for these children. And while it's true that it can be detrimental to children to give them too many material things, it's absolutely impossible to give a child too much love. Someone sent me a little clipping—I have no idea where it's from—that made this point so clearly. It said:

> Extra love from grandparents goes into a child's psychological bank account, which draws interest and can be used for an emotionally rainy day.

What a comforting thought—to imagine our grandchildren facing some tough decision someday or feeling lonely in some far-off place and suddenly remembering a grandmother's love—and being comforted by it. Surely there's no greater legacy we can leave to our grandchildren than this constant, enduring gift—the kind of love modeled by Jesus and described so beautifully in 1 Corinthians 13: a love that never ends.

GRANDPARENT: A thing so simple, even a small child can operate it.[6]

If you want to be loved,
don't criticize those you want to love you.[7]

Bouquets of Gold
"Grandma, I have flowers for you."
She held them up for me to view.
I took them from her little hand
And vaguely tried to understand
Emotions stirred anew.

Leafing back through 40 years,
A yellow meadow scene appears.
The little girl from whom I grew
Picked flowers for her grandma, too . . .

Glowing hemispheres.

Did Grandma pause and meditate,
Like me, begin to contemplate,
Recalling scenes with etched designs
When she picked golden dandelions
According to childish trait?

And will my grandchild someday hold
A bright bouquet of meadow's gold
Placed there by one as yet unborn?
And will she then recall this morn
And this story be retold?

Adeline Wiklund[8]

How far you go in life depends on your being
tender with the young, compassionate with the
aged, sympathetic with the striving, and tolerant of
the weak and the strong—because someday in life
you will be all of these.

George Washington Carver

Kids are like sponges.
They absorb all your strength and leave you limp.
Give 'em a squeeze, and you get it all back.

Bumper sticker: DON'T BUG ME! HUG ME![9]

A young boy, some six years old, was studying
his grandmother. Soon he asked, "Grandma, are
you a lot older than my mom?"

"I sure am, honey, lots older," she replied.

The boy nodded. "I figured that," he said, "but I
got to tell you that her skin fits a whole lot better
than yours."[10]

Grandma Brown took her two grandchildren to the zoo. . . . They stopped before a huge cage of storks. Grandma told the two youngsters that these were the birds that brought both of them to their dad and mom.

The two children looked at one another, then the oldest leaned over and whispered in his sibling's ear, "Don't you think we ought to tell Grandma the truth?"[11]

Life is like riding a bicycle.
You don't fall off unless you stop peddling.[12]

A grandmother took her three-year-old granddaughter into her lap and began reading to her from Genesis. After a while, noticing the little girl was unusually quiet, the grandmother asked, "Well, what do you think of it, dear?"

"Oh, I love it!" answered the child. "You never know what God is going to do next!"

Another grandmother took her four-year-old granddaughter, Amanda, to the doctor's office because she'd been running a fever. The doctor looked in her ears and said, "Who's in there, Donald Duck?"

Amanda said, "No!"

Then the doctor looked in her nose and said, "Who's in there, Mickey Mouse?"

Again Amanda answered, "No!"

Finally he put his stethoscope on her heart and asked, "Who's in there, Barney?"

Amanda replied indignantly, "No, Jesus is in my heart. Barney is on my underwear!"

Even when I am old and gray,
    do not forsake me, O God,
till I declare your power to the next generation,
    your might to all who are to come. (Ps. 71:18)

MENacing MENstrual Cramps, MENopause, MENtal Failure . . . Is There a Connection Here?

Men are like parking spaces.
All the good ones are already taken—and the rest are
handicapped or their meters are running out!

Bill was reluctant to let me replace our old, flattened bed pillows, but I finally talked him into it. We had had them for several years, and even when they were washed and dried, they were still too FLAT to suit me. They had lost their newness, and I insisted they needed to be replaced.

He wasn't eager to get new ones because he likes his bed pillow all squashed down and not puffed up. He clung like a child to his old, matted-down pillow, but the old ones didn't LOOK good and I kept insisting we needed new ones. Finally, he gave in.

I found some pillows on sale, and they were just terrific— big, fancy, blown-up poufs that looked really nice when the bed was made up. They weren't sagging and squashed down like the old flattened out ones.

Well, I was really proud as I carried those old, sorry-looking pillows to the trash can and stuffed them down into the bag that lined the can. But Bill didn't share my joy. He complained that he couldn't sleep because his new pillow was "too hard, too big, and too uncomfortable."

Since I was the one engineering this big transfer, I hated to admit it, but I woke up with a crick in my neck, too, and felt as though I'd been sleeping on a pile of rocks. It was sure hard to admit that perhaps I'd made a mistake in replacing those old, soft eiderdown pillows that had served us so well for many years. Bill was right. The new ones *were* too stiff. They wouldn't mold to our heads and necks the way the old ones did.

After two nights of this disturbed sleep (and after listening to Bill's continuing complaints) I knew I had to make the situation right . . .

By now the old pillows that I'd stuffed into the trash were buried under a couple days' accumulation of other garbage, and our garbage truck comes through our neighborhood early in the morning. So after the second sleepless night, I sneaked out of the house right at dawn and tiptoed out to the trash can, which Bill had set out on the curb the night before. Still dressed in my housecoat and slippers, I gently lifted the noisy lid off the can—then gasped as the stench of a week's collection of trash escaped from the container.

Where we live there are lots of older people who get up with the sun and go for morning walks. I knew I would have to take the risk that being caught digging through those bags of trash would earn me the neighborhood nickname of "BAG LADY." But I was a woman on a mission!

Hurriedly I tried to undo the little twistie on one of the bags. Bill always puts them on so tight, as though worried that something in there would try to ESCAPE! Well, I completely dug through that first bag of garbage, and it wasn't there—but in going through all the refuse, I'd spilled a bunch of OTHER trash. (Bill really packs a lot of trash in each bag because he's so neat about how he collects his trash, flattening every milk carton and cereal box and sometimes even tearing up the cardboard into little pieces!)

It took awhile, but after an eternity of pushing and shoving through the trash, I finally decided which bag the pillows were in. By this time, several couples had walked past me and nodded good morning (looking rather astonished to see me knee-deep in refuse).

Finally I pulled out both pillows, which were now stained with drops of grape juice, bleach droplets, and who knows what else, and hugged them to my heart. They felt so soft and comforting!

I dashed inside and immediately dropped both of them in the washer with LOTS and LOTS of soap (still moving as quietly as I could, mind you, so Bill wouldn't know what I had done).

Then I put them in the dryer with LOTS and LOTS of fabric-softener sheets. Of course, the dryer had to go through several cycles to get them dry because down and feathers take a LONG time to dry—nearly six hours in this case!

Finally they were dry, and I slipped them into the pillow-cases and remade the bed, really proud of myself that I had done all this without Bill's ever knowing what was happening.

It was dark that night when he finally climbed into bed and fell asleep, never realizing the switch that had been made.

The next morning as he was making up the bed (this is one of his little ways of showing love—he always makes the bed for me), I figured that he must surely know what I'd done. But he said not a word. As he finished up, he smoothed the bedspread over the pillows and said, "Well, you know, I guess those new pillows are okay. Maybe it just takes awhile to get used to them."

When he saw the crinkled smile I was trying to hide, I had to confess what I'd done. That old verse, "He that covereth his sins will not prosper" kept bouncing around my mind—and anyway, I was going to have to do some fast talking to explain why I had two BIG new pillows taking up a whole shelf in our closet. So I told him about diving into the trash can the day before. ("Oh," he said, a rather worried look on his face. "Did you get it all put back in the bags okay? Did you remember to put the twistie on tight?")

Anyway, now we have nice, matted-down, well-worn, OLD pillows, but they are COMFY and he is WUMPHEE (my long-time nickname for him), and we have one more thing to laugh about as we lay our weary heads on those old, familiar pillows each night.

"Look, I know you hate it, but until I get a chance to put some non-slip decals in the tub, I'd feel a lot better if you'd just wear the helmet."

Growing Old Together

If you've read my other books, you know I like to poke fun at men. Please understand that these jokes and anecdotes and wisecracks have nothing to do with FACT! They're just for fun. And since this book is FOR WOMEN ONLY, I want to add an extra helping of silliness here to celebrate these creatures God gave to us so we'd always have something to laugh about!

And just so you know, I love and respect Bill, my husband and soulmate through DECADES of fun and adventures. He's always been my anchor as well as the wind in my sails, whichever one I needed most at the time!

We work together well, and I'm blessed by his love and companionship. We've helped each other survive so many challenges that the other day, when I saw a startling scene, I thought it depicted our relationship perfectly. In the street before me, a tow truck was towing another tow truck.

Picture the strong person in your midst, the one you would call if you had a problem, the one who encourages you and builds you up. If you're like me, that person is your husband.

But what happens when that stable force needs help himself? That's what Bill and I went through many years ago when he was disabled due to an almost-fatal car crash. Then, for a little while, I was the tow truck towing the tow truck. Now we're both back on track and going strong—and laughing every chance we get.

Men, Women, Old Age, and Technology:
A Dangerous Mix

Bill is always looking for little gifts for me. Last year he got me the best gift yet: a lava lamp! He knows that I love things that move and chime and light up, and this bright red lava lamp is the highlight of my Joy Room. I love watching it ooze and swirl around. It's so soothing and peaceful.

Even though it's rather a "new" invention (actually I think they're making a comeback after first appearing in the sixties), somehow my lava lamp reminds me of simpler times, when clocks ticked and tocked, dishwashers had two arms and two legs instead of four "cycles," and telephones came with built-in helpers whose voices greeted you as soon as you gave the bell a crank: "Number please!"

The truth is, technology has just about left me behind. But the amazing thing is that it's leaving Bill behind too. He's just as confused as I am about some of the new computerized "advancements."

I'm finding this is true for lots of folks in our generation. Age is the great leveler when it comes to coping with advancing technology. It used to be when we couldn't figure out how to run some gadget or gizmo, we could call our husbands and they'd size up the situation in no time, press a few buttons, and send us on our way. But that's changing.

No longer are we the only ones who can't figure out how to turn on the air conditioner in a hotel room—or even to get into the room in some places with computerized locks! Now things are so complicated some husbands can't figure them out, either! One woman told me her husband bought a new large-screen television that came with a SIXTY-FOUR-PAGE instruction manual! (And we know what he did with that, right? Used it as a coaster.)

The woman said, "By trial and error, he learned how to turn it on and change the channel—and didn't even attempt to learn the zillions of other things this monster can do."

Maybe the problem is that these machines are rushing us, leaving us feeling disconcerted. Maybe that's why we can't catch on (or catch up!). A few years ago, *Parade* magazine published a little table of listings that explained why we no longer have time to catch our breath and figure things out. Technology is pushing us to do everything faster and faster— just when most of us would be content to snooze along on the SHOULDER of life's highway, stopping occasionally to smell the flowers—and sip some tea!

The table in *Parade* was titled, "The Vanishing Pause,"[1] and it looked like this:

SLOW MOTION	CRUISE CONTROL	FAST FORWARD
buttons	zippers	Velcro
stove	pressure cooker	microwave
washboard	wringer-washer	washer-dryer
pen	typewriter	word processor
abacus	adding machine	calculator
operator	rotary dial	touch-tone
U.S. Mail	Federal Express	fax

Looking at these lists, you can start to understand why so many of us older folks feel so tired all the time. We no longer have the tried-and-true excuses we used to use when something wasn't ready when it was expected. That's certainly been true for me since I began writing books. It used to be that if I didn't have a manuscript in to the publisher on exactly the deadline, I could say, "Oh, it must have been held up in the mail. I mailed it on . . . let's see, was it Tuesday or Wednesday?" when the truth was I hadn't gotten it into the mail until FRIDAY! Now when things are due on Friday, the publisher sends me a form for OVERNIGHT SHIPPING—or worse yet, a FAX NUMBER! So when something is not on time, I can't blame anyone but myself!

One woman told me she and her husband were planning a cross-country trip in their elaborate motor home and were hoping their eight-year-old grandson would come with them for part of the trip. "He's the only one who can program the satellite dish and figure out how to run the microwave," she confessed.

And even some of the younger husbands are having trouble with all the new-fangled gadgets on the market these days. At a meeting I attended recently, I met Bryan Eckelmann, a wonderfully warm and delightful minister in Massachusetts who has given me permission to share his hilarious story:

It was the first spring of my life away from the suburbs—a small farming community in Ohio. Timberly, my farm-savvy wife, eager to plant a big garden, was thrilled when one of the church members loaned us his roto-tiller.

After he dropped it off, Timberly raved, "Bryan, this isn't just any roto-tiller, this is the best—a Troy-Bilt Pony!"

I tried to act impressed and educated at the same time. "Yes, I know. I've seen them in the magazines."

I *had* seen the ads praising this tiller's power and ease of use. The words were always accompanied by a photo of a woman in an A-line skirt effortlessly guiding the tiller around the garden with only her index finger. What could be easier!

So easy that I was happy to help. Our infant son had colic and was only happy in the front pack Timberly wore *while* she tried to run the tiller. After one long row and an aching back, she asked me to finish the job when I came home.

No problem! I changed clothes and got to it.

But no guiding this tiller with one finger for me—after one hour I was hot, aching, and cursing false advertisers everywhere. I had only tilled two rows when Timberly came out and asked, "What's the problem?"

"It's just slow going," I yelled over the engine roar of this two-hundred-pound monster. "This isn't working well at all—maybe something's broken." I was trying to act brave, but she knew I was exasperated.

"Broken? It can't be! We just borrowed it!" Timberly stepped behind the machine, reached down to a lever I had not seen before, and pulled up. The tiller lurched forward under its own power.

Shocked, I yelled, "How'd you do that?!"

She stopped the machine and stared at me for a moment, both of us taking in the fact that I'd spent an hour *pushing* a two-hundred-pound self-propelled tiller around our garden without engaging the driver mechanism. For three months both of us were too embarrassed to tell a soul!

Bryan, being the fine pastor he is, was quick to apply his roto-tilling lesson to his ministry: "That day was a great lesson for me," he said. "Since then, I've come to recognize those all-too-frequent times when I've tried in vain to push and pull my life in the right direction, ignoring the limitless power of God's Spirit so easily available to me, His child."

It's about time men experienced some of the technological torture we women have faced for so long! Actually, I agree with something Erma Bombeck wrote many years ago. She said, "Men have a reputation for being mechanical. This is not true. Occasionally, Christmas has to be postponed while a man in a closet tries to put together a bicycle, following instructions (in Japanese) and looking for the E wing nut."[2]

"I couldn't afford to get airbags as an option. If it looks like we're going to hit something, start blowing these up."

Car Trouble

Bryan's story reminds me of how silly my sister and I felt when we borrowed a friend's car during a weekend conference in another state. It was a very nice car, just the right size and easy to drive, but throughout the long weekend we were unable to get the windows to roll down. There seemed to be lights and colors and levers for everything else, but there was no button to roll down the windows.

We returned the car on Sunday, and as we were thanking the owner, I happened to mention that we hadn't been able to find the button to lower the windows.

"Oh," she said, surprised. She opened the car door and pointed to a rounded crank in front of the armrest. "It's right here—you just turn this handle."

Janet and I, both accustomed to power windows, had been looking for a button to push when the BIG lever to roll the windows down manually was RIGHT THERE! We had probably bumped it a dozen times as we were feeling around, trying to find the button. We laughed until we cried, thinking how "modern" we were when all that was needed was a little old-fashioned common sense!

Last year I had a similar "splash of joy" when I was speaking in North Carolina at the church Billy and Ruth Graham attend. What an honor it was when Ruth Graham called the place I was staying and invited me to go to church with her.

Billy was out of town and her car was in the repair shop, so she came to pick me up in his car. She immediately explained all that to me and apologized for not being familiar with the rather elaborate controls. In fact, she had to speak over the blaring of the radio because she didn't know which knob to turn to get if off—and of course I was no help. The car is specially equipped with phones and security devices, so just a small thing like turning off the radio seemed to be a big deal—at least to us non-mechanically inclined women!

Soon another problem became obvious. It was an unusually warm day, and the car was getting hot. Ruth asked me to turn on the air conditioner while she was driving to the church. I looked at all those little knobs and gizmos and couldn't read ANY of the tiny letters identifying each one. Hesitantly, I tried pushing one lever across a slot, but it quickly became apparent that instead of turning on the air conditioner I had accidentally revved up the HEATER!

Finally, Ruth stopped the car, and we asked a passer-by if he could turn off the heater and get the air conditioner going for us. It must have been a funny sight: two mature women, pulling up to the curb with the radio blasting and heat pouring out of the car. We both had some good laughs about how ridiculous we felt that day; it really broke the ice (in more ways than one!) and made getting acquainted a joyous experience.

Deceiving Tendencies

Space-age technology isn't the only thing that puts us old-age men and women on the same level. It seems to me there are many ways that men and women mellow out and become more alike, more compatible, as we toddle off toward the sunset. One article said that becoming grandparents often enriches a couple's marriage and gives their relationship a new depth. In other situations, the relaxed pace of traveling together with no schedule, no itinerary, gives retired couples a new sense of shared adventure.

For Bill and me, our work with Spatula Ministries and all the traveling we do to far-flung speaking engagements has given us a new purpose in life. The boomerang joy we receive as we meet new people all over the country has enriched our lives beyond measure.

One of the things Bill and I do together is the monthly shopping. Someone once said, "The only thing worse than going shopping with a husband who doesn't like to shop is going shopping with a husband who DOES like to shop!" Because he's a retired engineer, Bill can really get into the DETAILS of shopping, comparing prices and carefully deciding which is the best buy. It used to drive me nuts when I was always in a hurry, but now that our lives are a little more relaxed, I enjoy having him along.

Recently we were at one of the big warehouse stores; somehow we got separated, and I came out ahead of Bill while he was occupied with something else in the store, and for a change I pushed the cart to the car and unloaded it (a job he always does for me). When we got home and I began to put things away, I realized I had apparently LEFT two huge boxes of stuff in the bottom of the cart! We had shoved them onto the bottom of the cart, and apparently I had just overlooked them as I transferred our purchases from the cart to the car.

When I told him what had happened, he just said, "Well, it's down the drain now. You can consider that stuff totally lost." His pessimistic opinion frustrated me so much that I decided to drive the fifteen miles BACK to the store just to show him he was wrong.

Bill refused to go with me, pooh-poohing the idea that I would ever find those lost boxes. "Why bother?" he asked. "You're just wasting your time—and gasoline too."

But I was thinking to myself, *If I don't get the stuff back (which I probably won't) I will just go back in and purchase every-thing again and tell Bill I found them after all!* He would never know the difference, I rationalized, and I would have the great satisfaction of proving him wrong.

This thought persisted as I got closer to the store; I began mentally plotting my route up and down the aisles, collecting all the lost items, re-buying them, and then bringing them home and letting him think I had miraculously FOUND them.

When I pulled into the crowded parking lot and started to make my way to the entrance of the store, I must have had a frantic, searching look in my eyes because when I stopped a cart boy and hesitantly began to explain my problem (*couldn't hurt to ASK*, I reasoned), he immediately said, "Oh, you're the lady who left the big boxes in the bottom of the cart. They're inside the store. We have a whole closet full of things people leave in their carts and we keep them there, safe and sound."

Astonished, I sputtered, "Does it happen THAT often?"

"Oh yeah," he replied. "We have a lot of people who drive off and leave stuff in their carts." He smiled at me and added, "But they're usually OLD PEOPLE."

Well, that made my day! After loading my stuff in the car, carefully making sure this time that I hadn't left anything in the cart, I drove home wondering whether I should be flattered or humiliated by the boy's remark. Then I thought about my plan to re-buy all the stuff I thought I'd lost and never let Bill know what I'd done. That verse from Jeremiah kept popping into my head: "The heart is deceitful above all things, and desperately wicked" (17:9 KJV). Yet, I had to admit it would have been a lot more fun to pull that kind of prank rather than just returning home and saying, "Look what I found!"

The sad part is that when Bill saw me coming in with all the stuff, he said, "I'll bet you just went back and re-bought all the stuff to make me look bad!"

Pretending to be shocked that he would even *have* such a thought, I denied—at least for a little while—that I would even consider such a scheme.

Men are wonderful creatures; they truly are. They compliment us—and complement us! They can make us cry; they can build us up—or leave us flattened. They support us and nurture us and console us. In short, they're nice to have around! But one of their most valuable gifts to us women, in my rather lop-sided opinion at least, is that they give us so much to laugh about. Here are some of my favorite quips and jokes about our struggles with the new technology—and especially about men. If you are married, it might be better to enjoy this little collection while he's out playing golf or getting the car tuned-up!

An elderly gentleman went to the doctor for a health checkup. The doctor gave him a good going-over then pronounced him in fine shape.

"So, how do you stay so healthy?" the physician asked him.

"Doc, God is with me day and night," the old gent replied.

"That's nice," the doctor replied, hardly looking up.

"No, Doc. I mean He's with me *everywhere* I go. Even at night, when I get up out of bed to use the bathroom, God is right there to help me. He even turns the light on for me."

"He turns the light on for you?" the doctor asked, puzzled.

"Yep! Every night when I go to the bathroom, God turns the light on for me."

The doctor stepped into the waiting room to speak privately to the old man's wife.

"Your husband seems to be in good health physically," the doctor said. "But he might be slipping mentally. He said something peculiar. He said God Himself turns the light on for him when he gets up in the night to use the bathroom."

"Why, that old coot!" the wife retorted. "He's been piddlin' in the refrigerator again!"

"I'm a walking economy," a man was overheard to say. "My hairline's in recession, my waist is a victim of inflation, and together they're putting me in a deep depression."[3]

Generally speaking, men and women respond to situations quite differently.

Ask a man where he got a cake, and he'll tell you, "At the grocery store." Ask a woman the same question, and she'll ask, "What's the matter with it?"

But ask a woman how she bruised her toe, and she'll say, "I kicked a chair." Ask a man the same question, and he'll reply, "Somebody left a chair in the middle of the room!"[4]

Growing old is only a state of mind . . . brought on by gray hairs, false teeth, wrinkles, a big belly, shortness of breath, and being constantly and totally pooped.[5]

Men don't really lose their hair—
it just goes underground and comes out their ears!

Morning memory jog, upon arising:
It's gotten so I have to put a sign beside my bed:
"First the pants, THEN the shoes!"[6]

Youth looks ahead,
Old age looks back,
Middle age looks TIRED.[7]

Lewis and Clark were not really meant to explore the West for all those months. They simply did not want to admit (especially in front of Sacajawea) that they were lost.[8]

An eighty-year-old lady was complaining to a friend that she had a lot of trouble during the night because a man kept banging on her door. When her friend asked, "Why didn't you open the door?" the lady replied, "What? And let him out?"[9]

Dave Barry's advice on how to drive like a geezer:

1. The geezer car should be as large as possible. . . . If necessary you should get TWO cars and have them welded together.

2. You should grip the wheel tightly enough so

that you cannot be detached from it without a
surgical procedure, and you should sit way
down in the seat so that you're looking directly
ahead at the speedometer.

3. You should select a speed in advance—23
miles per hour is very popular—and drive
this speed at all times, regardless of whether
you're in your driveway or on the inter-
state. . . .

4. If you're planning to make a turn at any point
during the trip, you should plan ahead by
putting your blinker on as soon as you start
the car.[10]

Two ninety-year-old men, Herb and Herman,
were at the funeral service for another ninety-year-
old pal. After the benediction, they lingered, looking at the open casket of the deceased brother.
Finally, Herb said to Herman, "You know, it's hardly
worth going home."[11]

Congressman Claude Pepper, at age eighty-seven:
"At my age, I don't even buy green bananas."[12]

In buying a gift for your wife, practicality can be
more expensive than extravagance.

Max Lucado[13]

Have you ever wondered why it takes MILLIONS of sperm and only one egg to make a baby? Maybe it's because not one of those little surfers will stop and ask for directions!

Gary Smalley[14]

Father

4 years: My daddy can do anything.

7 years: My dad knows a lot, a whole lot.

8 years: My father doesn't know quite everything.

12 years: Oh, well, naturally Father doesn't know that, either.

14 years: Father? Hopelessly old-fashioned.

21 years: Oh, that man is out-of-date. What did you expect?

25 years: He knows a little bit about it, but not much.

30 years: Maybe we ought to find out what Dad thinks.

35 years: A little patience. Let's get Dad's assessment before we do anything.

50 years: I wonder what Dad would have thought about that. He was pretty smart.

60 years: My dad knew absolutely everything!

65 years: I'd give anything if Dad were here so I could talk this over with him. I really miss that man.[15]

The perfect man met the perfect woman, and they got married. One Christmas Eve, they were driving down the highway and noticed a man stranded by the side of the road. This was no ordinary man. It was Santa Claus!

Being the perfect people they were, they offered Santa a ride because he was in a hurry to get his toys delivered. Alas, the roads were slippery, and there was a terrible car crash. Two of the three people were killed. Do you know who survived?

(The perfect woman. Everyone knows Santa Claus and the perfect man don't really exist.)

Author and pastor Max Lucado says he used to be a "closet slob" with the attitude, "Life is too short to match your socks; just buy longer pants!"

Then, he says, he got married![16]

CURE FOR BALDNESS IN MEN
Epsom salts
Persimmon juice
Alum

Combine all ingredients and rub mixture on head daily. (It won't keep your hair from falling out, but it shrinks your head to fit what you have left!)

Getting a husband is like buying an old house. You don't see it the way it is but the way it's going to be when you get it remodeled.

Do you know what a dirty old man is?

A middle-aged father with three daughters and one bathroom!

A retired husband is a wife's full-time job.[17]

Jesus was walking on the water and came up to a boat with three men fishing. As Jesus climbed into the boat he saw that one of the men wore thick glasses and had poor vision. Jesus took the man's glasses and threw them into the water. As soon as they hit the water the man's eyesight was restored.

The next man held out a withered hand. Jesus touched his hand and the man's flesh was restored.

Jesus then turned to the third man. The man held out his hands and said, "Lord, don't touch me! I'm on disability pension!"[18]

A friend who is bald says he will *never* wear a turtleneck sweater. He's afraid he'll look like a roll-on deodorant!

This is the same friend who said he used to use Head & Shoulders—but now he needs Mop & Glow!

After a canceled flight at an unspecified airport, passengers mobbed the reservation counter. Airline personnel were doing their best to rebook passengers quickly. But a demanding passenger pushed to the front of the line, pounded on the counter, and shouted repeatedly, "You have to get me on this plane."

The reservations agent remained accommodating and unrattled.

The passenger's tirade became even more incensed and insulting. "Do you know who you're talking to?" he shouted. "Do you know who I am?"

The agent calmly took the microphone and announced over the intercom, "Ladies and gentlemen, we have a passenger here who doesn't know who he is. Will someone who knows this passenger please come identify him?"

And with that, the other passengers broke into applause.[19]

Mirth is God's medicine. Everybody ought to bathe in it. Grim care, moroseness, anxiety—all this rust of life ought to be scoured off by the oil of mirth. It is better than emery. Every man ought to rub himself with it. A man without mirth is like a wagon without springs, in which everyone is caused disagreeably to jolt by every pebble over which it runs.

Henry Ward Beecher

Rebuke a wise man and he will love you.
Instruct a wise man and he will be wiser still; teach a
    righteous man and he will add to his learning.
The fear of the LORD is the beginning of wisdom,
    and knowledge of the Holy One is understanding.
    (Prov. 9:8–10)

Ready for Liftoff!

I'm a child of the King . . . still living in
palace preparation mode.

Last year I was honored to be a guest in the home of a very wealthy woman. As we pulled into the driveway, I was amazed at the size of her beautiful mansion. It rose elegantly from the carefully manicured grounds, a stately structure with a wide, columned porch that opened into a foyer featuring a grand, winding staircase. Standing at the front steps I had to lean way back and rest the back of my head on my shoulders just to see the top of the house.

Frankly, I was a little intimidated by the size and opulence of this majestic home. But then a uniformed maid opened the front door for us, and there was our gracious hostess, welcoming us with outstretched arms and a warm heart and making us feel right at home in the luxurious surroundings.

She showed us around, and each room was more beautiful than the one before it. Finally, she guided us into a grand dining room, where the table was set with some of the prettiest china I had ever seen; in fact, someone told me later this woman had several different sets of exquisite china.

Everything in her home was lavish, from the crisp linen napkins and glittering silverware to the dainty dessert plates and the sparkling chandelier.

It was lovely, but as I sat there in the vast dining room, enjoying our hostess's hospitality, the words to that old, old song drifted into my mind: "A tent or a cottage, why should I care? He's building a PALACE for me over there."[1]

It was all I could do to keep from blurting out suddenly, "You know, I'VE GOT A PALACE TOO!"

Actually, Bill and I now live in a comfortable mobile home.

"I'm getting so old that all my friends in heaven will think I didn't make it."

But we've got a MANSION waiting for us in heaven—and I'm dancing on tiptoes in my eagerness to get there!

Recently I've started collecting angels—but not just *any* angels. I collect trumpet-tooting Gabriels! They're everywhere around our home—little ceramic figurines and colorful banners depicting angels dressed in flowing gowns, mighty wings majestically spread. And each one holds a long, slender horn. Everywhere I look I see an angel and that little joke I saw somewhere comes to mind:

> DUE TO THE SHORTAGE OF
> TRAINED TRUMPETERS,
> THE END OF THE WORLD
> WILL BE POSTPONED THREE MONTHS!

Well, if all my angels could suddenly become real, there would certainly be no shortage! They're there to remind me of that joyful day when Gabriel will sound his horn, and we'll all move into our mansions in heaven. On that glad moving

"A Child of the King" by Marilyn Goss

day, we'll slip into our heavenly robes, adjust our heavenly crowns atop our heads, and hurry eagerly, arms outstretched and faces aglow, toward our heavenly Host: Jesus! Won't it be fabulous to have Him show us around and point out which mansion is our own!

Imagining that day, I picture heaven as a place filled with beautiful mansions that glow like the light-filled homes in artist Thomas Kinkade's radiant scenes. Have you seen his work? It's . . . well, it's heavenly! He has an incredible talent for creating scenes that are both splendid and inspiring. Light seems to spill out of the homes' windows and doorways, reminding me of that line that says:

> Sunset is heaven's gate . . . ajar.

Having Thomas Kinkade's lovely pictures in my home, along with all my happy angels, keeps me constantly filled with joyous anticipation of what's waiting for me in heaven. These reminders keep me focused on what's REALLY important in this life. They help me remember the message my friend Dick Innes put in the form of these inspiring words:

> **Time**
> We enter it at birth.
> We pass through it in life.
> We exit it at death.
> It was our preparation for eternity.

Until that day comes and Gabriel blows his horn, we're living in palace preparation mode, folks!

When my editor saw the theme of this chapter, she said, "But Barb, you wrote about that in your LAST book."

My answer was, "Yes, I did. But the Lord hasn't come yet, has He? So we're STILL living in palace preparation mode!"

Don't ever forget it! Our life here is nothing more than preparation for the next one. Surround yourself with reminders of that heavenly promise.

The angel figurines scattered in every room of our home and the striking Thomas Kinkade pictures hanging on my walls do more than hint of heaven; they reassure me that none of my problems are here to stay. As the Bible says, they "came to pass"! No matter what trials beset me here, I've got a reservation in a much better place.

A luxurious palace is waiting for me. My name is already painted on the mailbox! The lights are on, and the table is set. (Just think of that when you hear the quip, "Death is God's way of saying, 'Your table is ready'!") And best of all, the Lord Himself is standing in the doorway, waiting to welcome me! One of these days, I'm gonna move in there and spend eternity in glorious praise of the One who created it all for me.

What a happy day that will be! Thinking of it reminds me of that little Christian comment that says:

> When I was born, people were happy and smiling. I was the only one crying.
> When I died, people were sad and crying. I was the only one happy and smiling.

When I go, I'm going out with a laugh. No matter what my outward appearance, you can believe on the inside I'll be singing and shouting hallelujah. It won't be anything like the little item someone contributed to the newsletter published by Joel Goodman, director of the Humor Project. It said:

> I work on an obstetrical floor in a hospital. Someone recently posted an article at our nursing station which said, "Recent research shows that the first five minutes of life are very risky." Underneath that, someone else had penciled in the words, "The last five minutes aren't so hot either!"

As Christians, we can LAUGH at death. For us, death is not the joyless end of our lives; it's the *beginning* of endless joy.

Our final exit here will be our grandest entrance there! That encouraging fact is the lifeline we cling to every day of our lives; it's the secret that empowers us to face with courage *anything* that comes our way because we know (1) God is with us; we're His; we're engraved on the palms of His hands, and (2) better days are ahead—if not in this life then in the next. As someone said,

> For Christians, *nothing* is the end of the world!

Dying to Get to Heaven

When Bill and I were meeting recently with our insurance agent, he consulted some actuarial tables and told me my life expectancy was another nineteen years. The poor man probably expected me to be a little sad to hear this prediction. I was sad, all right, but not in the way he expected. As he delivered this bit of news, my face automatically wrinkled up into a frown, and I spouted off, "Ugh! I don't wanna wait *that* long!"

It's not that I'm living a miserable life. On the contrary, I've made it a habit to wring out of every single day all the fun and love I can find. Sometimes it seems I have the best of both worlds—overflowing joy here and the promise of eternal happiness in paradise. Still, I know that my pleasantest day here on earth is *nothing* compared with the unfathomable joy that awaits me in heaven.

Someone told me about an elegant fashion show organized several years ago by a church women's group. The guests were rewarded with several door prizes, and one frail but spirited ninety-year-old lady burst into laughter as she opened the gift she'd won—a *twenty-year* goal-planner. Shaking her head and laughing happily, she quickly handed it to a much younger woman at her table. "Honey, I hope to heaven I won't be needing this!" she said with a merry twinkle in her eye.

That woman didn't need a place to write down her goals for the next twenty years; at that point her main goal was arriving at heaven's gates and moving into her mansion—and her new, perpetually youthful body!

No Luggage Allowed

Can you imagine how glorious our lives in heaven will be? No, probably not—it's simply beyond our comprehension. Heaven will be so wonderful that the material things we cherish most on earth will be meaningless because our days will be filled with an exuberant joy that comes merely from being in God's presence.

Have you heard the story about the rich man who was determined to "take it with him" when he died? Here's how it goes:

> [The] rich man prayed until finally the Lord gave in. There was one condition: he could bring only one suitcase of his wealth. The rich man decided to fill the case with gold bullion.
>
> The day came when God called him home. St. Peter greeted him but told him he couldn't bring his suitcase.
>
> "Oh, but I have an agreement with God," the man explained.
>
> "That's unusual," said Saint Peter. "Mind if I take a look?"
>
> The man opened the suitcase to reveal the shining gold bullion.
>
> Saint Peter was amazed. "Why in the world would you bring pavement?"[2]

When we're heading for a place where the streets are paved with gold, we won't need to bring any carry-on items! Someone once said, "The only thing we can take with us is the love we leave behind." That's so true.

Lifting Up Others with Love

Where does this love legacy come from? When we welcome Jesus into our lives, He fills our hearts with love—packed down, overflowing. Then we invest it in others—and our investment multiplies!

Several years ago, I saw an essay by J. Anne Drummond that pointed out how "the real treasures, the lasting treasures, are not here on earth. The ones that matter are those that are stored in heaven. . . . One day all the keepsakes we store in the backs of our closets will be taken by our loved ones to save in *their* closets or sold to someone else or thrown away. But the treasures of love and personal friendship with Jesus Christ can never be taken from us."[3]

In my childhood home, a plaque hung on the wall to remind all of us, "Only one life, 't will soon be past. Only what's done for Christ will last." Somehow those lines still help me today to get a better perspective on my life here on earth and remember that what we do in this short life counts toward ETERNITY! We can't take anything WITH us, but we can send love on ahead—by sharing Christ's love with those who are in need here.

Noteworthy Encouragement

One of the ways we share God's love is through encouragement. Someone said the word *encourage* means "to fill the heart, to puff it up, to enlarge it." By encouraging a friend, we give that person a special gift—a boost that is aptly described in this little essay by an unknown writer:

> One of the most powerful things one person can share with another is *encouragement*. Encouragement can stop a suicide, a divorce, and countless other tragedies. A word of encouragement can heal someone who is broken and wounded. It can give someone the courage to keep trying. . . .
>
> The people of God should be a radiant contrast to the people of the world. We should bubble over with the joy of the Holy Spirit. We should find it easy to be positive and uplifting. Are you an encouragement to those around you? Don't let someone die from neglect and lack of encouragement. Share your Christian joy!

Our sin-tainted world delights in discouragement; negative people pollute our outlook and weaken our hope. But Christians know the antidote for discouragement; it's spelled out again and again in Scripture: "Anxious hearts are very heavy but a word of encouragement does wonders!"[4] The address book from my old college days is imprinted with this reminder: "As cold waters to a thirsty soul, so is good news from a far country."[5] When others write to encourage me, I reread their notes several times before depositing them in my Joy Box—to be read many times in the future.

So many hearts need to be filled up with hope. As I speak around the country, I look out over the audiences and imagine hearts that are squashed down, stamped on, flattened out from lack of care or from thoughtless deeds done to them, or shriveled and dying from lack of encouragement. What happiness it brings ME to share a glad word with those hurting hearts and help bring restoration with an infusion of God's hope! When something is restored it pops back in place, like an out-of-joint bone that is popped back into alignment, relieving the pain. Encouragement works like an emotional chiropractor—and both "doctor" and patient benefit from the treatment. As someone said, "Encouragement is a double blessing. Both giver and receiver are blessed."

Becoming an Encourager

It's easy to be an encourager. We can encourage someone with a cheery phone call, a quick visit—or just a smile. One of my favorite ways to encourage others is by writing a quick note. Usually I jot something down on a silly cartoon I've seen somewhere. The message doesn't have to be long. Brief and sincere notes can uplift the receiver as much as a bouquet of flowers—perhaps more. If you find it hard to express yourself, begin by telling your friend about some kindness she has done for you. Remind her how much her friendship means to you, then offer your own encouragement to her.

Note-writing has always been a part of our family life. Perhaps that's why the little "Memo from Jesus" at the front of this chapter means so much to me. Like the angel figurines and the Kinkade pictures, copies of this memo are posted around my house to remind me Jesus is coming back for me.

We had as our guest a young man from Canada who lived with us for a year while he attended high school. He came from a rather uncommunicative family, so it took awhile for him to get used to our family's constant chatter and joking— and especially to all the notes we left each other.

The boys had learned always to check the refrigerator for notes from me. Typing has always been faster than handwriting for me, so I would type out the list of chores I expected of each of them. Even though I tried to divide the work evenly, one day Larry complained that he had too much on his list. "I'll *never* get all this stuff done!" he pouted.

When we compared all the boys' notes, the problem quickly became apparent. Barney, who was then ten, had redone all the notes, laboriously retyping them (with one finger) and redistributing all of HIS chores to his three brothers! Then he signed the notes "MOM" and even put on some of my lipstick and blotted his lips to imprint a "kiss" on the notes, just as I always did!

Luckily, our Canadian guest missed out on this prank. Before he returned home he said the *one thing* he really loved about living with us was our "note system." He said getting a note telling him what chores were expected of him, where everyone was, what to do to prepare for dinner, and what activities were planned for that evening was like having his own private mail system.

A Gift of Hope

An encouraging note can mean a lot, even to those who are accustomed to receiving them. Mark Twain, who was known to be a vain man, confessed that he could "live for three weeks on a single compliment."

Encouragement is the gift Chuck Swindoll describes as a "hope transplant" to someone in need.[6] Erma Bombeck was a talented encourager. For decades, she encouraged millions of us as she simultaneously entertained us with her syndicated newspaper column and her books. She kept on encouraging and entertaining us right up until the end. When she died last year, the whole nation paused to reminisce at the love and laughter she had shared. One writer described her as "a national treasure in a world and age that desperately needs to lighten up."[7]

Erma was one of my role models. We met—briefly—only one time, but she touched my life—and the lives of millions of others—through her words, her humor, and the Christian kindness she showed to all who knew her. She encouraged others to wrap themselves in happiness and to endure hardships by focusing on the "big picture" rather than getting bogged down in drudgery. One of her best columns, published several years ago, described how she would do things if she could live her life over:

> There would have been more I love yous . . . more I'm sorrys . . . more I'm listenings . . . but mostly, given another shot at life, I would seize every minute of it . . . look at it and really see it . . . try it on . . . live it . . . exhaust it . . . and never give that minute back until there was nothing left of it.[8]

Many would say that Erma, by her writing, helped us live the way she said she would have relived her own—with gratefulness for the blessings right under our noses. And finally, there was Erma's farewell. Published in her last column just five days before she died, it was used to introduce her last book, *Forever, Erma*. It said:

> My deeds will be measured not by my youthful appearance, but by the concern lines on my forehead, the laugh lines around my mouth, and the chins from seeing what can be done for those smaller than me or who have fallen.[9]

If *my* spirit is wrinkled and lined, I hope those crinkles are from being pressed against God. That's where I've tried to stay throughout my life, no matter what circumstances beset me. As Hudson Taylor said, "It doesn't matter how great the pressure is. What really matters is *where the pressure lies,* whether it comes between me and God or whether it presses me nearer His heart."[10] Romans 8:39 says this so clearly: "NOTHING can separate us from the love of God." He *WALLPAPERS* our hearts to His.

Nothing can happen to us in this life without coming through God's filter. As someone said, citing Romans 8:18, "Heaven's delights will far outweigh earth's difficulties." Whatever we must endure here is only temporary. When God permits His children to go through the furnace experiences of our lives, He keeps His eye on the clock—and His hand on the thermostat!

This life is only temporary; it's the next one that lasts forever. We have only a few allotted years between eternities to do God's work here on earth. As someone said, "Heaven will mean the most to those who have put the most into it." While we're here in God's waiting room, living in palace preparation mode, each of us has a role to play, a job to do.

Some save lives; others save souls.

Some raise children; others comfort the dying.

Some feed the hungry; others clothe the poor.

Some help the needy; others encourage the fearful.

Many times in my life, I've been lifted out of a cesspool by others' kind, encouraging words; in their notes and voices I have heard God speak. When I landed on the ceiling, God handed others a spatula of love to scrape me off and send me on my way again.

And then it was my turn. God set me down on the shores of the cesspool and handed me the lifeline I now gladly throw to others. The lifeline is God's loving encouragement, which pulls us into God Himself.

Clinging to one end, I throw the other end to someone who's recently landed in the muck. And then God lifts both of us out of the cesspool and wraps us in His comfort blanket of love.

Sharing Heaven's Hope

There is *nothing* in your life that God and you cannot handle together—if you get out of the way and let HIM be in control. He can turn your troubles into blessings, and then He can use those blessings to add depth to your spirit so that your praise for Him is even more fervent and joyous and your life is an inspiration to others.

My friend Rose Totino, founder of Totino's Frozen Pizza, lived that kind of inspiring life. She faced a lot of challenges during her seventy-nine years. But she never took her eyes off heaven. In fact, when I look at the enthralling photograph of Rose on the next page, I see a marvelous joy radiating from that exuberant smile, don't you? That sparkle of joy we saw in Rose was the reflection of God's glory.

This photograph was used by American Express in an advertising campaign featuring American heroes. Several years later, it was printed again in a much more touching way. It appeared on the front of the leaflets given to guests at Rose's memorial service in 1994. Inside the leaflet, the tribute to Rose noted how she would want to be remembered: "as a woman whose face was always turned to God and as one who knew so well that when the day came for Jesus to take her home, there would be, as she often said, 'no U-Haul behind the hearse.'"

This was followed by a beautiful little essay—one Rose had spotted on a bulletin board at the Mayo Clinic. It said:

> Cancer is limited.
> It cannot cripple love.
> It cannot shatter hope.
> It cannot corrode faith.
> It cannot eat away peace.
> It cannot destroy confidence.
> It cannot kill friendship.
> It cannot shut out memories.
> It cannot silence courage.
> It cannot invade the soul.
> It cannot reduce eternal life.

It cannot quench the Spirit.
It cannot lessen the power of the resurrection.

Author Unknown

Many beautiful words have described Rose, but it is the photograph that touches my heart most deeply. It's as if, in that ecstatic smile, Rose is responding to the joyously welcoming chorus she hears as she nears heaven's gates.

For Rose—and for all Christians—death isn't something to be feared. It's precious! It's our grand entrance into heaven, our arrival at the foot of God's throne. What a happy time that will be! When I think of the joy and peace that await me there, I can hardly wait!

Rose W. Totino
Photo reprinted with permission of the American Express Corporation.

Permission Acknowledgments

Mail addressed to Spatula Ministries arrives by the basketfuls, and each day's letters bring new anecdotes, cartoons, poems, jokes, and maxims my thoughtful friends have clipped or quoted from unidentified magazines, newspapers, church newsletters, and bulletin boards. Many of these little gems are too good not to share—but in many cases, despite diligent effort, I've been unable to identify the original source. Please contact the publisher if you can help identify the creators of these little treasures so that proper attribution can be given in future printings.

As always, I especially appreciate the help of those writers, agencies, artists, and friends whose names are listed below. They have graciously agreed to share with me—and with you, the reader—something they created in order to give all of us a little boost.

American Express Corporation and the Rose Totino family for allowing me to reprint the inspiring photograph of Rose that concludes the last chapter of this book.

Ashleigh Brilliant of Brilliant Enterprises, 117 W. Valerio Street, Santa Barbara, California 93101, for his clever Pot-shots that are sprinkled through the book.

Ruth Harms Calkin for sharing her poem "Suddenly Mine" in chapter 4.

Mary Chambers and InterVarsity Press for the funny cartoon in chapter 8.

J. Anne Drummond for allowing me to quote from her essay "Estate Sale" in chapter 8.

Gallant Greetings for letting me reprint the greeting card in chapter 3.

Randy Glasbergen for sharing five of his clever cartoons that appear throughout these pages.

Marilyn Goss and Arts Uniq' for Marilyn's beautiful rendering of "A Child of the King" in chapter 8.

Dr. Robb Hicks, Dick Innes, Sue Nichols, Dorothy Petersen, Rev. Larry Potts, Marilyn Shilt, Rev. Roger Shouse, and Sherrie Weaver for sharing their anecdotes, jokes, poems, and experiences with the readers of this book.

Nancy L. Jackshaw and Leaning Tree Publishing for sharing the witty lines from one of the company's greeting cards.

The *Kansas City Star* for permission to reprint the Schorr cartoon in chapter 4.

Bil Keane for sharing one of his clever "Family Circus" cartoons in chapter 6.

The King Features Syndicate for Wayne Stayskal's "Ralph" cartoon in chapter 2.

Ann Landers and Creators Syndicate for the delightful letters from her column that appear in chapter 4.

Meadowbrook Press for allowing me to use cartoons from Jane Thomas Noland and Ed Fischer, *What's So Funny about Getting Old?* and Mary McBride, *Grandma Knows Best But No One Ever Listens!*

John McPherson for generously sharing four silly cartoons in chapters 2, 3, and 7.

Pamela Pettler for sharing "The Stress Diet" in chapter 2—and a special thanks to the Pettler family members scattered coast to coast who helped me find Pamela.

The nice folks at Recycled Paper Greetings for letting me reprint in chapter 2 that dancing fat lady from one of their clever cards.

Dana Summers for his witty cartoons in chapters 1 and 4.

TON Communications for allowing me to use the words from an "It's in the Bible" greeting card in chapter 4.

Universal Press Syndicate for efficiently granting my requests to use an item from a "Dear Abby" column and for these cartoons and comics: "For Better or For Worse" by Lynn Johnston, "Real Life Adventures" by GarLanco, and "Tight Corner" by Grundy/Willett.

Sherrie Weaver for again sharing her clever witticisms scattered throughout the book.

Adeline Wiklund for allowing me to reprint her touching poem "Bouquets of Gold" in chapter 6.

Notes

Chapter 1. The Wonder Years

1. Dorothy Parker, quoted in Lois L. Kaufman, *Old Age Is Not for Sissies* (White Plains, N.Y.: Peter Pauper Press, 1989), 57.
2. Bill Cosby, quoted in Kaufman, Ibid., 55.
3. Dave Barry, *The World According to Dave Barry* (New York: Wings, 1994), 237.
4. Verla Gillmor, "Managing Menopause: Help and Hope for Facing the Change," *Today's Christian Woman,* January 1997, 49.
5. Dr. Harvey Austin, quoted in Kaufman, *Old Age Is Not for Sissies,* 42.
6. Rob Scott and Mike Wallard, designers, *Girls Just Wanna Have Facelifts: The Ugly Truth about Getting Older* (Kansas City, Shoebox Greetings, 1989).
7. This description appeared in an excerpt from Gail Sheehy, *Silent Passage* (New York: Random House, 1992), in the *Austin American-Statesman* Lifestyle section, 16 June 1992, D-1.
8. Margaret Mead, quoted in *Family Circle,* 14 May 1996, 52.
9. Marilyn Meberg, *Choosing the Amusing: What Difference Does It Make?* (Portland, Oreg.: Multnomah, 1986), 24.
10. From a Sylvia greeting card © Nicole Hollander and © The Maine Line Company, Rockport, Maine.
11. Lady Nancy Astor, quoted in Erma Bombeck, "At Wit's End," 15 February 1995, the *Orange County Register* Accent section, 5.
12. Robert Fulghum, *Uh-Oh: Some Observations from Both Sides of the Refrigerator Door* (New York: Villard, 1991), 184.

13. Norene Firth, *A Bowl of Cherries: Looking at Life Through Homespun Homilies* (Norwalk, Conn.: The C. R. Gibson Co., 1980).
14. Martin A. Ragaway, *Don't Even Think of Retiring Until . . .* (Los Angeles: Prince/Stern/Sloan, 1982).
15. President Dwight Eisenhower, quoted by Jacquelyn Benfield in a column titled "Age Clues" in an unidentified newspaper clipping sent by a friend of Spatula Ministries.
16. Roger Rosenblatt, "Secret Admirer," *Modern Maturity*, August 1993.
17. Sherrie Weaver, *Stress or Insanity* (Glendale Heights, Ill.: Great Quotations, 1996).
18. This Scripture verse and Nancy L. Jackshaw's clever line are part of a beautiful greeting card published by Celebration Greetings, Boulder, Colorado. Used with permission.

Chapter 2. Fat Farm Failures . . . and Other Excuses for the Middle-Age Spread

1. Associated Press, "Thin may be in, but fat's where it's at," *St. Petersburg Times*, 16 October 1996, 1A.
 2. Pam Pavlik's "Upfront" column in the *Philadelphia Inquirer*, "The real skinny," date unknown.
 3. Erma Bombeck, *A Marriage Made in Heaven* or *Too Tired for an Affair* (New York: HarperCollins, 1993).
 4. *Tampa Tribune*, 25 September 1996, Baylife 2.
 5. Pamela Pettler, "The Stress Diet" in *The Joy of Stress* (New York: William Morrow, 1984). Reprinted with permission.
 6. Chef Leonardo DiCanio, quoted in "A Taste of Gold," *Tampa Tribune* Food & Health section, 5 September 1996, 1.
 7. Mary Anne Cohen, director of the New York Center for Eating Disorders, quoted in *Tampa Tribune* Baylife section, 23 September 1996, 2.
 8. This little quip appeared on—what else?—a refrigerator magnet by Linda Grayson, produced by Printwick Papers.
 9. Fitness trainer Chris Reichart, quoted in *Tampa Tribune* Business & Finance section, 11 March 1996, 4.
10. "Veggies That Taste Like Fruit?" *Tampa Tribune* Baylife section, 20 September 1996, 2, citing an article in *Child* magazine.
11. *Tampa Tribune*, 27 June 1996.
12. Bernice Kanner, "Americans admit lying is a daily habit," Bridge News, reprinted in the *Tampa Tribune*, date unknown.

13. Taken from a Dear Abby column by Abigail Van Buren. Distributed by Universal Press Syndicate. Reprinted with permission. All rights reserved.
14. *Weight Watchers Little Book of Wisdom: Words to Lose By* (Weight Watchers International, 1987, 1995).
15. Thanks to pastor Larry Potts, First Christian Church, Gainesville, Missouri, for sharing this insight.
16. Sherrie Weaver, *365 Days of Life in the Stress Lane* (Glendale Heights, Ill.: Great Quotations Publishing, 1994).
17. Weaver, *Stress or Insanity.*

Chapter 3. A Fact of Aging: What You Lose in Elasticity You Gain in Wisdom

1. WHO definition of fitness, cited in Susan H. Thompson, "Benefits of exercise are easy to attain," *Tampa Tribune*, 5 September 1996, 3.
2. My Joy Room started out as a shoebox-size Joy Box that I quickly outgrew. For details, see my book *Stick a Geranium in Your Hat and Be Happy* (Word, 1990).
3. Dr. James Rippe, *Fit Over Forty* (New York: William Morrow, 1996).
4. "Vitality, Vim, and Vigor, Six Steps to More Energy," a pamphlet published by the Baylor College of Medicine Office of Health Promotion, One Baylor Plaza, Houston, TX 77030.
5. Eugene F. Ware, quoted in John C. Maxwell, *Leadership 101: Inspirational Quotes & Insights for Leaders* (Tulsa: Honor Books, 1994), 34.
6. Dave Barry, *Stay Fit and Healthy Until You're Dead* (Emmaus, Penna: Rodale, 1985), 15.
7. Ibid., ix–x.
8. "Don't just stuff and veg," *Tampa Tribune* Food and Health section, 26 September 1996, 3.
9. Fitness expert Candice Copeland-Brooks of Mammoth Lakes, California, in a *Living Fit* article quoted in "Get on the ball," *Tampa Tribune* Food and Health section, 26 September 1996, 3.
10. Randolph Schmid, the Associated Press, "Feeling Your Age a Matter of Mind," undated clipping sent by a friend of Spatula Ministries.
11. Adapted from William Van Wert, *What's It All About?* (New York: Simon & Schuster, 1996), 128.

12. Sanford University School of Medicine Psychiatrist William F. Fry, cited in "Fit notes," *Tampa Tribune* Food and Health section, 14 November 1996, 6.

13. From a cartoon by Randy Glasbergen. Used by permission.

Chapter 4. Growing Old Is Inevitable; Growing Up Is Optional

1. Associated Press, "Clinton praises Lucid's space feat," 28 September 1996.

2. Larry Laudan, *The Book of Risks* (New York: Wiley & Sons, 1994), cited in Jeffrey Kluger, *St. Petersburg Times*, 9 June 1996.

3. Max Lucado, *He Still Moves Stones* (Dallas: Word, 1993).

4. Carol Kent, *Speak Up with Confidence* (Nashville: Thomas Nelson, 1993), 47.

5. Ingrid Trobisch, "Losing a Loved One," *A Better Tomorrow Magazine*, Winter 1993, 89.

6. Adapted from Alfred A. Montapert, "Ten Steps to Brighten Your Life." Publishing source unknown.

7. Reported by Charles Osgood, "Newsbreak," CBS. Radio Network, 22 September 1980.

8. *Tampa Tribune*, 17 September 1996.

9. Ibid.

10. Marc Silver, *U.S. News & World Report*, 4 June 1990, 76.

11. Millard and Linda Fuller, *The Excitement Is Building* (Dallas: Word, 1990), 34–35.

12. Ann Landers, 13 December 1995. Permission granted by Ann Landers and Creators Syndicate.

13. Sherwood Eliot Wirt, *I Don't Know What Old Is, But Old Is Older Than Me* (Nashville: Thomas Nelson, 1992), 87.

14. Dave Veerman, ed., *How to Get Along with the Opposite Sex: Book 2 of the Ready for Life Series* (Wheaton, Ill.: Victor Books/ Scripture Press, 1994).

15. Donna Watson, Ph.D., *101 Ways to Enjoy Life's Simple Pleasures* (Austin, Tex.: Bard and Stephen, 1994), 17.

16. H. Jackson Brown Jr., *Live and Learn and Pass It On* (Nashville: Portal Publications, 1992).

17. From an "It's in the Bible" greeting card, the copyright of TON Communications Inc., Newark, Delaware. Used by permission.

18. This funny story was submitted by Janice S. Walsh to "Lite Fare," *Christian Reader*, September–October 1996, 76.

19. "Suddenly Mine" from *Lord, You Love to Say Yes* by Ruth

Harms Calkin, Pomona, California. Used by permission. All rights reserved.

Chapter 5. Precious Memories—How They Leave Us

1. Ravi Zacharias, *Deliver Us from Evil* (Dallas: Word, 1996).
2. Van Wert, *What's It All About?* 230.
3. Hugh O'Neill, *New Choices* magazine, October 1996, 72.
4. Ibid.
5. Charlotte Davis Kasl, Ph.D., *Finding Joy: 101 Ways to Free Your Spirit and Dance with Life* (New York: HarperCollins, 1994), 84–85.
6. The story of Bill's accident and miraculous recovery is told in *Stick a Geranium in Your Hat and Be Happy*.
7. This little gem was credited to *Railway Employees Journal* in an unidentified clipping sent by a Spatula Ministries friend.
8. Weaver, *365 Days of Life in the Stress Lane*, October 1.
9. Adapted from Weaver, ibid., August 31.
10. Martin A. Ragaway, *Good News, Bad News* (Los Angeles: Price/Stern/Sloan, 1984).
11. Bill Cosby, quoted in Kaufman, *Old Age Is Not for Sissies*, 56.
12. Erma Bombeck, *Star News*, Hendersonville, Tennessee, 12 November 1993, 2A.
13. Ed Fischer and Jane Thomas Noland, *What's So Funny About Getting Old?* (Minnetonka, Minn.: Meadowbrook Press, 1991).
14. Adapted from a joke in "Laughter, the Best Medicine," *Reader's Digest*, April 1996, 77, and combined with other contributions sent by friends of Spatula Ministries.

Chapter 6. Grandmothers Are Antique Little Girls

1. Bombeck, *A Marriage Made in Heaven*.
2. Max Lucado, *A Gentle Thunder* (Dallas: Word, 1995).
3. "35 years behind baby boomer bottoms," *St. Petersburg Times*, 8 September 1996, 6H.
4. Adapted from "Grandma, Let's Play," *A Better Tomorrow* magazine, winter 1993, 74–77.
5. John Crudele, CSP, and Richard Erickson, Ph.D., *Making Sense of Adolescence* (Liguori, Mo.: Triumph Books, 1995), quoted in *Servant Life*, February 1996, 5.
6. Adapted from Charles L. Allen, *Grandparents R Great* (Uhrichsville, Ohio: Barbour, 1992), 8.

7. Ibid., 60.
8. Used with permission of Adeline Wiklund, Shelley, Idaho.
9. Jack Canfield and Mark Victor Hansen, *Chicken Soup for the Soul* (Deerfield Beach, Fla.: Health Communications, 1993), 12.
10. James E. Myers, *A Treasury of Senior Humor* (Springfield, Ill.: Lincoln-Herndon Press, 1992), 180.
11. Ibid., 181.
12. Ibid., 173.

Chapter 7. MENacing MENstrual Cramps, MENopause, MENtal Failure . . . Is There a Connection Here?

1. "The Vanishing Pause," *Parade* magazine, 16 February 1992, 23.
2. Erma Bombeck, "Erma Bombeck's Life Secrets. For such a young person, I've learned a whole lot," *Family Circle*, September 1982, 60.
3. Milton Segal, quoted in "Quiplash," undated column from *Christian Reader*.
4. Martha J. Beckman, *Meditations to Make You Smile* (Nashville: Dimensions for Living, 1995), 117.
5. Original source unknown. Adapted from Allen, *Grandparents R Great*, 48.
6. Attributed to "RTN" in Fischer and Noland, *What's So Funny About Getting Old?*
7. *Over the Hill: Humorous Thoughts on Growing Older* (Lombard, Ill.: Great Quotations, 1986), 33.
8. Adapted from Weaver, *365 Days of Life in the Stress Lane,* June 9.
9. Lucille Nahemow, Kathleen A. McCluskey-Fawcett, and Paul E. McGhee, eds., *Humor and Aging* (San Diego: Academic Press, 1986), 114.
10. Barry, *The World According to Dave Barry,* 275.
11. Reggie the Retiree, *Laughs and Limericks on Aging—in Large Print* (Fort Myers, Fla.: Reggie the Retiree Co., 1991).
12. Kaufman, *Old Age Is Not for Sissies,* 8.
13. Max Lucado, *When God Whispers Your Name* (Dallas: Word, 1994), 43.
14. Gary Smalley, *Making Love Last Forever* (Dallas: Word, 1996).
15. This essay appears in Ann Landers, *Wake Up and Smell the Coffee!* (New York: Villard, 1996) citing the Danbury, Conn., *News-Times* and a Dutch magazine.
16. Max Lucado, *In the Grip of Grace* (Dallas: Word, 1996), 116.

17. Kaufman, *Old Age Is Not for Sissies*, 62.
18. Thanks to Roger Shouse, Indianapolis, Indiana, for sharing this little joke.
19. Adapted from a Knight-Ridder Newspapers article appearing in the *Tampa Tribune* Baylife section, 25 June 1996, 2.

Chapter 8. Ready for Liftoff!
1. Harriett E. Buell, "A Child of the King," 1877.
2. The Rev. Warren Keating in *The Joyful Noiseletter*, reprinted in *Reader's Digest*, December 1995, 63–64.
3. J. Anne Drummond, "Estate Sale," *Decision* magazine, September 1986. Used by permission of J. Anne Drummond.
4. Prov. 12:25 TLB.
5. Prov. 25:25 KJV.
6. Charles Swindoll, *Hope Again* (Dallas: Word, 1996).
7. *National Catholic Reporter*, 10 May 1996, 2.
8. Erma Bombeck, "At Wit's End." Used by permission of the Aaron Priest Agency.
9. Erma Bombeck, *Forever, Erma* (Kansas City: Andrews and McMeel, 1996), xiv.
10. Hudson Taylor, quoted in Swindoll, *Hope Again*.